WASHINGTON IN PIECES

Washington

in Pieces

JOHN NOLLSON

Doubleday & Company, Inc., Garden City, New York
1981

ISBN: 0-385-15413-5
Library of Congress Catalog Card Number 80–713

Grateful acknowledgment is made for the following:

"A Little Bit of Soul," originally entitled "Soul," and "The Real CIA," originally entitled "A Spy in His Cups," both copyright © 1977 by Alternative Magazine; "The Quiet Revolution," originally entitled "Aspen; The New Rome," "Music Hath Charms," originally entitled "Mideast Countdown," and "Interim Report," all copyright © 1978 by The American Spectator; "Haiku on the Issues," originally entitled "Laconique Politique," "Washington Whirlaround," originally entitled "Washington's False Faces," "The Great White Whale," originally entitled "Call Me Ahab," "Lost Names," originally entitled "A Nation of Irvings," "The Commanding Heights," originally entitled "PLO on the Potomac," "Fiction," originally entitled "Amalgamated Political Fiction," "Politics on Tap," and "Drink American," all copyright © 1979 by The American Spectator.

For my long-suffering little audience

CONTENTS

INTRODUCTION

The material in this book was originally submitted as a doctoral dissertation to the faculty of political science at Monash University in Melbourne, Australia. It was rejected. Now, thoroughly edited and revised, it has been published with a new introduction. For this, I wish to acknowledge the advice and support of my great-uncle, Sir Kenneth Nollson, the well-known Australian jurist, who encouraged me in the completion of this task, and who is pledged to offer his counsel in the event of lawsuits.

The reader may wonder why it is necessary to undertake yet another re-examination of the political and social structure of Washington, D.C. It is necessary because we are approaching the end of an era. It is an era which began sometime in the early 1950's when, for the first time, Americans learned it was possible to send out for pizza. It is an era which closes with the discovery that pizza is carcinogenic. But within these broad parameters, there are many parts of the landscape which need to be filled in, many concave places which must be fleshed out, many vague boundaries which must be framed up. I cannot claim to have finished these tasks, and I hope

that others will feel compelled to complete their own mono-
graphs on these matters.

I wish to acknowledge further my great debt to both the
"new criticism" and the "new history." Without these pioneering efforts, my own work could not have been initiated, and
certainly not completed. Several new critics and many new
historians have read this work in various stages, and their suggestions have been invaluable to me. The manuscript has also
been read by a few new journalists, but their suggestions were
useless and have been ignored. Overall, I have received a
large number of evaluations of this work. Most of them were
without merit and were totally irrelevant. I have been able to
disregard all of them, and this book is much the better for it.

The research and writing were undertaken wholly at my
own expense. Though I applied to several learned societies for
financial support, none was forthcoming. I visited several libraries in various different places, and received no special assistance. In the main, I found the personnel in the libraries I
consulted to be very uncooperative and, more often than not,
just plain surly. Their charges for the use of copying machines
were also exorbitant. Thus, so far as the final product is concerned, the good and valuable things in it result almost exclusively from my own labors. Whatever flaws remain are the
fault of those who deliberately refused to help me. A perfect
example of this is the postgraduate student hired to prepare
the index. A third of the way into it, he quit in order to take
up a better-paying position. No one volunteered to take his
place.

This book has been divided into three parts in order to represent the eternal triad of the human experience, namely,
God, Man, and Yale. This triad is sometimes designated "thesis, antithesis, synthesis," or "Father, Son, and Holy Ghost," or,
more familiarly, "bunking, debunking, and rebunking." But
they are all the same thing, and they meet at the Apex.
Though many friends and advisers have criticized this pyra-
midical structure, they will just have to live with it.

Ordinarily, a book of this scope could not have been completed without the active inspiration of the author's own family. Yet, as the work wore on, my wife and children grew increasingly uncooperative and unsupportive. Their initial reluctant acquiescence gave way rather quickly to censure and neglect, and ultimately to malicious acts of sabotage. It is a remarkable tribute to my own persistence that I was able to persevere despite their implacable hostility. Indeed, they exhibited not one wit of tolerance, understanding, or forbearance. Even so, I am under court order to ensure that they share equally in the movie rights.

John Nollson

WASHINGTON IN PIECES

Book I

MANY ARE CALLED,
BUT NONE IS CHOSEN

Open City

He had begun as the Totally Unknown One and had become, in quick succession, the Front Runner, the All-But-Certain Nominee, and the Virtually Elected One. Now, he was the Newly Elected One, and he was climbing into the limousine. It had been brought out onto the runway of Washington National Airport to greet his airplane. Only five members of the twelve-man welcoming Committee could be crammed into the back seat with him. He made the decisions with characteristic boldness, and the unlucky seven were obliged to hitch rides further back in the motorcade.

He was in an expansive mood. "This is my fourth trip to Washington, as I recall—one in each of my three previous incarnations—and now as the Newly Elected One. This time, I'd like to see a few of the sights, but I don't want to inconvenience anyone. I'll just leave it all in your hands."

"Oh, it's no bother at all," said the five, almost in unison. "We want you to have a good time," one of them added.

By now, the limousine had reached the airport gate—where it was halted by a crush of young men wearing three-piece suits and carrying Samsonite attaché cases. They thrust their hands toward the car, and a few managed to press their faces against the car's windows. One struggled to get his bony hand through the front vent. His faint voice could be heard groaning, "jobs, jobs, Great One. What are a few jobs to one who is Newly Elected?" The Secret Service agents pulled him away.

"What's this all about?" asked the Newly Elected One.

"It's the beggars," said one of the Committee. "They're an eyesore and an embarrassment, and we have tried for a number of years to move them out of the city. But somehow—during lunch hour, I guess—they manage to get out to the airport and fall on the car of anyone judged to be among the Newly Elected."

"Yes, the beggars," said the Newly Elected One, "I've heard about them. Still, it's something of a shock to see them in the flesh right here in the Nation's Capital. And why do they have warts on their hands? Why, they're under better control in New Delhi! When I visited Mrs. Gandhi, there wasn't a beggar in sight. Would one of you make a note to do something about this?"

The five reached for their notebooks almost simultaneously. "Doesn't like beggars," they wrote.

The limousine continued down the road but, after three more miles, it was halted once again, this time by a makeshift wooden barrier. In front of the barrier stood the Archbishop of the City in his splendid robes, wearing a miter and carrying the traditional shepherd's crook. Behind him were several hundred nuns, arranged in rows of ten. Each was saying a rosary.

The Newly Elected One and his associates stepped out of the car and approached the barrier. The Archbishop raised his right hand and made the sign of the cross.

"Bless you, my son," said the Archbishop. "I have heard that your followers are now within sight of the city. News of your conquests precedes you."

"Yes," said the Newly Elected One, "and it certainly is neighborly of you folks to come out and meet me. I appreciate it."

"I am somewhat relieved to discover," said the Archbishop, "that you have some of the social graces. I, of course, am just a simple pastor who cares only for his flock. Their welfare is my first concern. Yet, I am also concerned for the priceless treasures of this old city. I propose to ransom them."

"Of course," said the Newly Elected One. "I am not ignorant of the history of the Church. Didn't something like this happen when Attila the Hun was at the gates of Rome?"

"Precisely," said the Archbishop. "The Holy Father reminded us of this episode in his most recent pastoral letter. That is why I am authorized to pay you one million ounces of gold if you agree that this city will not be sacked—an amount equal to the unexpended balance of your opponent's campaign fund."

"I appreciate your concern," said the Newly Elected One, "but you needn't worry. I don't have a single Hun among my followers," he continued good-naturedly. "Most of them are Baptists."

"Unhappily, my son," replied the Archbishop, "this is a distinction which is lost on the Holy Father. As much as I have explained the difference to him, I do not believe he apprehends it. I wish, therefore, to set his mind at ease, so I implore you to accept the million ounces. Let there be commerce between us."

"Let me assure you," said the Newly Elected One, "that no one in the city has anything to fear. After all, the temporal authorities agreed to negotiate a peaceful surrender. They were even willing to come out to my railroad car to sign the final instruments, but I decided it was a needless bother. Nonetheless, I agree to accept your gift—which will be used only to retire the campaign debt. Convey my best wishes to the Holy See, and tell the Curia there's no cause for alarm."

"I shall pray for you, my son," said the Archbishop and, once again, he made the sign of the cross. Then he motioned to the nuns to clear a path for the limousine.

"*Ite, missa est*," he intoned.

His campaign debt thus retired, the Newly Elected One and his party re-entered the limousine and resumed the ride. "Make a note," said the One, "that the Church's entitlements are to be respected."

"Respect Church's entitlements," they all scribbled.

As the motorcade drove on, the hosts pointed out several items of interest along the way. "This is your intelligence agency," said one. "This is your Pentagon," said another. "This is the Watergate building, which contributed so much to your success," said a third. "This is Arlington Cemetery," said a fourth, "where we would be happy to begin work on a magnificent tomb for you, if you like."

"That's not necessary," said the Newly Elected One curtly.

By now, the party had reached the broad thoroughfare which connected the White House and the Capitol. As they drove toward the Capitol, they could see the festive crowds which lined the street. People strained to catch a glimpse of the chief occupant of the limousine. Government officials leaned out of the windows of their offices. They were cheering and waving white handkerchiefs.

"What unanimity," said the Newly Elected One. "I'm very encouraged."

"To be honest," said one of the Reception Committee, "there were some who were less than pleased by the recent turn of events. They have already left the city and have vowed to carry on an underground Resistance movement. A few small cells already exist in scattered law firms and a handful of universities. As for the Resistance, who can tell who is a member and who isn't? Should you ever be overthrown, many of those cheering you now will let it be known that they were part of the Resistance all along."

"I have heard similar stories," said the Newly Elected One. "I have met many who were part of the Resistance which formed during the rule of the Tyrant. One must respect those people. It is easy to join the Resistance formally so that you can make a big thing of it later. Obviously, it is far more difficult to feign collaboration when in fact you are part of the Resistance. Isn't it wonderful to learn that, during the reign of the Tyrant, everyone was part of the Resistance except the Tyrant himself?"

"This guy still has a lot to learn," they all wrote in their notebooks.

The limousine reached the steps of the Capitol, and music, flowers, and prayers were offered in proper sequence. The Speaker of the House escorted the Newly Elected One to the House Chamber, and the Newly Elected One addressed the representatives of the people.

"Do not think of yourselves as a conquered people," he said. "You have not been occupied; you have been liberated!"

They applauded.

"Moreover," he continued, "some say I have come to this Capital seeking glory, power, and riches."

"No, never!" they shouted in unison.

He raised his hand, and quiet was restored.

"I am grateful for your vote of confidence in my humility," he continued. "Yet, I am a realist. I know that some of you will betray me, but I wish all of you could have been my running mate nonetheless!"

They cheered wildly.

That night, the Newly Elected One slept in the home of one of his early supporters. He rose early, made his own bed, and resolved that, if he ever needed a night out on the town, he would definitely visit the new Hyatt-Regency. "Make a note," he said to one of his aides. "In view of the willingness of the inhabitants of the city to cooperate, we will lift the siege of the city and allow the resumption of shipments of liquor and tobacco."

And so it began.

Senator Wimbol

It had frequently been said of Senator Larethan Jerome Wimbol that if he did not already exist, it would have been impossible to imagine him. And once more, it was time for that hexennial ritual, wherein Wimbol would again stand in the well of the Senate and take the oath of office. It was the twentieth time he had done so, and it made not a ripple. In truth, the beginning of even his fifteenth term had also gone unnoticed. That he had now served one hundred and fourteen years as a United States senator was a fact of nature. His service had commenced at age thirty-two, and he was now one hundred and forty-six; if he lived through his current term, he would attain the age of one hundred and fifty-two.

Wimbol himself played down his enormous age. "If I lived in the Caucasus, or in Ecuador, or in Peru, survival to this degree would appear unexceptional," he had said on his one hundred and thirtieth birthday. And, he had added with a patriotic huff, "there is no reason to believe that I should *not* have lived this long. The American system of free enterprise and mixed economy ought to promote longevity at least as effectively as state socialism or primitive tribalism." Besides, it was no longer interesting that, on each birthday, Wimbol would lapse into a discussion of some event or personage of the preceding century that no other living American could still recall. Thus, his one hundred and tenth birthday was more widely noted than his one hundred and twentieth. Wimbol began to wonder whether anyone was interested in his remarkable survival.

Along about age one hundred and twenty-seven, however, Wimbol's life had taken on a new purpose. For he had become anathema to a rising group in America, the "Topsies," as they called themselves. The Topsies took their name from the immortal poem "Thanatopsis" by William Cullen Bryant, and they formed the most militant wing of the Right to Death Movement. No Topsy wanted to live much beyond age fifty; indeed, according to their own bylaws, death by age fifty-three was mandatory; if a member were still alive at that age, he or she was immediately expelled. The Topsies lived hard and played hard, so that few among them had ever faced the ignominious choice between expulsion and suicide. For the Topsies, Wimbol's endless existence was a moral outrage. It was not so much that no one had the right to live so long; it was worse. No one had the right to *want* to live so long.

On Wimbol's one hundred and thirty-first birthday, three Topsy terrorists were gunned down by police in the hallway outside his office. A note found in the pocket of one of these would-be assassins made it plain that theirs was a "do or die" mission. The three—two women and a man—were already fifty-two and, by their lights, had little left to lose. "It is necessary to bring this worthless heel to a bad end before he becomes a sesquicentenarian," their press release had read. "We have come to invoke cloture on Senator Wimbol. We have come to postpone him indefinitely. We have come to recommit him to the Select Committee on Aging. We have come to table him. We vow that no man shall serve on the American

Revolution Quadricentennial Commemoration Commission
who also served on the American Revolution Tricentennial
Commemoration Commission." But they expired with their
slogan on their lips: "Life be not proud, though some have
called thee mighty."

Thereafter, this test of wills between Senator Wimbol and
the Right to Death Movement became one of the enduring
themes of American politics. Wimbol made his plans and organized his defenses. He hired three bodyguards and a food
taster. He followed a different route to the office every day.
He studied the Oriental martial arts and took to showing
Bruce Lee movies in his home. He trained himself to sleep but
three and a half hours a day.

Wimbol's arrogance was matched by Topsy determination.
They tried to zap him with a laser beam installed on the roof
of a building opposite his office. They placed a small atomic
bomb they had hijacked in the basement of the building, but
it was discovered and defused just in the nick of time. They
mailed him sausage high in nitrate content, in the hope he
would take a liking to it. They arranged for stewardesses to
give him complimentary packages of cigarettes whenever he
traveled. On "Tribute to Senator Larethan Jerome Wimbol
Day," organized by his grateful constituents, they arranged
through various front groups to buy and present to him a
Ford Pinto. Alone among the political activists in Washington,
D.C., they supported the construction of a massive nuclear
power plant in the inner city, in the hope that it would either
blow up or melt down. All the death-inducing devices of modern life were brought into play.

But Wimbol survived them all. And after each failed attempt, his colleagues would come to him in the cloakroom
and give him a slap on the back or a pat on the rump. "Atta
boy, Lareth!" they would say. Or: "Way to go, big fella!" Or:
"That's showing the bastards, Larry!" And both his colleagues
from the District of Columbia would never fail to clasp his
hand in the traditional soul shake and remark as how Wimbol,
for all his primitive political opinions, was nonetheless some
kind of hard-assed dude. Indeed, each such incident became

the occasion for long tributes, spoken on the floor of the Senate in praise of the distinguished gentleman. Invariably, one of Wimbol's colleagues would propose new appropriations to provide additional security devices for Wimbol's protection, and such measures would be routinely adopted without a single dissenting vote.

Repeatedly humiliated by Senator Wimbol's unshakable grasp on life, the Topsies were forced to re-evaluate their position and their tactics. For, after many years of inconclusive struggle, the issue between Wimbol and the Topsies had reached, so to speak, a dead end. Last April, three Topsies appeared in Wimbol's anteroom under a flag of truce to open negotiations. They proposed as their opening gambit that Wimbol agree to end his own life at age one hundred and sixty, in return for which all attacks on his person would cease. This the Senator rejected outright. They offered, next, to arrange for Wimbol to expire, at the same age, in the amorous embrace of a young mistress, so that he would depart this life with his reputation for chivalry and courage intact. This he accepted in principle, but proposed age one hundred and seventy-five as the deadline. This was unacceptable to the leaders of the Topsies, who, already in their mid-forties, would be long gone and unable to witness their ultimate triumph over the forces of hoariness. Thus stalemated, each party turned the negotiations over to its respective lawyers and, so far as the press knows, the bargaining continues apace. Last week, it was assumed that the discussions had reached a critical phase when a total news blackout was imposed.

Always one to confound the opposition, Wimbol arranged for his press secretary to leak a story that the Senator had purchased a retirement home in Arizona. But to his colleagues, he remained full of beans, assuring them that, at the right time, he would ask them to appropriate $280,000 for the biggest bicentennial birthday bash Washington, D.C., had ever seen.

The Real CIA

As I rode through the hunt country of northern Virginia not far from Washington, D.C., I realized that I had become separated from the rest of my mounted group. I sighted a small barn with an open door, a most inviting structure; perhaps it was a place where I might find some water for my thirsty horse. I approached, dismounted, walked in, and noticed immediately that the barn was no barn at all, but a refurbished vaulted room. Steel filing cabinets lined one wall, two long tables piled high with papers stood against another. My eyes were drawn to a long oaken table in the middle of the room where I noticed two gentlemen in what seemed to be British riding attire. They were drinking tea.

One of them, who bore an uncanny resemblance to Richard Burton, stood up to introduce himself. He thrust out his hand. "Leamas," he said, "Alec Leamas."

I was taken aback. "Not *the* Alec Leamas," I stammered,

"surely not *the* spy who came in from the cold! I thought John Le Carré had killed you off at the Berlin Wall back in 1964!"

"Yes," said Leamas with a tone of world-weariness, "the most poignant death in the history of espionage since the hanging of Nathan Hale. But unlike Mr. Hale, I am still very much alive. You must realize that Le Carré was working hand in glove with MI-5, part of a larger plan, you see. Reduction in force. But the upshot is that I have been kept on as a consultant. May I present my friend and colleague George Smiley."

"Smiley?" I blurted out, and surely I must have appeared thunderstruck. Here, in a nondescript, made-over barn was the legendary George Smiley, the same Smiley who had ferreted out the traitor in British intelligence, the Smiley who had flushed out The Mole. Smiley—still one of the few Englishmen who ranked with Robert Morley on the scale of patriotic commitment! What was George Smiley doing here?

"May I offer you some tea?" asked Smiley.

"Certainly," I said.

"Milk or lemon?" he asked.

"Milk will be fine," I answered.

Out of the corner of my eye, I noticed that Leamas had added neither milk nor lemon but had instead withdrawn from his hip pocket a small flask. He poured a generous amount of brandy into his teacup.

"Don't be disturbed by Alec," volunteered Smiley. "You see, ever since he was portrayed in the cinema by Richard Burton, he has acquired a taste for the theatrical, for the flamboyant. Indeed, when he has had too much to drink, he fancies himself as the famous actor altogether."

My mind was racing. Was it this which had brought Leamas to America, this strange transference, this desire to relive his greatest triumph? Did he think he was Burton? Did he know, as almost everyone did, that Elizabeth Hilton Wilding Todd Fisher Burton Burton Warner was now living in the very hunt country where Leamas, Smiley, and I were taking tea?

Somehow—perhaps it was his years of experience—Smiley

sensed my anxiety. "Our business here has been quite straightforward, really quite ordinary, run-of-the-mine MI-5 business," Smiley said reassuringly. He stared into his teacup and reached for a scone. "Our work is about done; we've been called home and we'll soon be packing up to go," he said.

"Yes," seconded Leamas, "about time to pack up, so near to Elizabeth, yet so far. All this time here, and we've not yet met." He poured more brandy into his teacup.

"It's getting to him," Smiley muttered, "too long out of being in the cold." He removed his glasses and began polishing them with a handkerchief. Then he cleared his throat.

"Ahem," said Smiley, "you are probably wondering why we are being so frank with you."

"Yes," I said, "from what I've read, it's not customary among spies to be so forthright."

"Fact is," continued Smiley, "we've been in your country on a mission, one that has already changed the history of the Western world. Two centuries ago, it was you Yanks with your revolution who turned the world upside down—as the old song had it—making the first crack in the Empire. Well, turnabout is fair play, eh? Poetic justice and all that."

"Bah," growled Leamas, "it takes George forever to get to the point. We've been experimenting with powerful behavior-modification drugs, that's what we've been doing. Wonderful things they are, and we've spread them about in prepackaged popcorn, in frozen Chinese food, in reconstituted wheat germ —everywhere."

I tried to absorb the import of what Leamas had just said. Was it true? Not a stone's throw away from the CIA's head-quarters I was sharing tea with two British agents—long thought to be washed up, one of them thought to be dead in fact—two British agents who, to speak honestly, were dressed in rather shabby tweed, but who had nonetheless managed to conduct behavior-modification experiments on a previously unimagined scale!

"Why, uh, why, may I ask, did you do all of this?" I asked haltingly.

"Ah," said Smiley, "to see whether we could infect you with it."

"With *it?*" I asked quizzically.

Leamas snickered. "The English sickness," he said casually, "just testing your susceptibility to the English sickness."

We fell silent.

It devolved on Smiley to break the awkward pause in the conversation. "You must learn," he said, looking directly at Leamas, "that you ought not to reveal Official Secrets, especially those having to do with the Yanks' competitive advantage and how we might try to reduce it."

"Oh," I volunteered cheerily, "no breach of security here! I've read all about Projects Artichoke, Bluebird, Chick-wit, and Mk. Ultra-delta. Gee, I never guessed that you Brits were clever enough to do all of that and tag it on the CIA!"

"You colonials are always underestimating us," Smiley chuckled. "I'm surprised your enterprising journalists have yet to figure it out. Surely, you are aware of the peculiar things that have been going on in your country these past dozen years?"

"Yes," interrupted Leamas, "it didn't start with Watergate."

"No, indeed, it did not!" said Smiley with an uncharacteristic note of assertiveness in his voice. "It began when they brought in as director of MI-5 someone with a red-brick university background—that's a Labour government for you—a fellow with one of those American-style degrees, Master of Industrial Progress or Doctor of the Post-Technotronic Era, or some such. Quite a change from Control, who had read medieval literature at Cambridge. We old individualists were slated for early retirement, another reduction in force. For some reason, though, we were put to work on this small project, perhaps because the new man didn't think it would amount to much. We've showed him, haven't we, Alec?

"You know," Smiley said, "sometimes these experiments can get somewhat out of hand, especially when under the direction of an irrepressible prankster like our friend Leamas. Well, sooner or later the whole story will come out, it always does. You see that Alec is quite a one for the brandy. It was back in '66, as I recall, that he was quite drunk, down in the dumps, moping about the old days in Berlin—when his eyes lit up. Yes, I remember what he said: 'I wonder what it would be like to take that uptight old bugger Nixon and turn him on with some acid?' Ever-resourceful Alec, that's why he was invaluable to us behind the Iron Curtain! He trailed Nixon to the bar of the Plaza Hotel and then and there laced his scotch and soda with a large helping of LSD! Uproarious flashbacks, what? For a time, we considered telling your Senate committees, but we couldn't devise a plan for dealing with the diplomatic difficulties. We are old allies, after all. Besides, my dear friend, how *could* we have known?"

Leamas' laughter had now reached the point of hysteria. The man was nearly convulsed. He pounded the table with evident delight.

Smiley stirred his tea once again and finished what was left with a quite audible gulp. "I suppose," he said with an air of resignation, "that this conversation constitutes a substantial violation of the Official Secrets Act."

"Bugger the Official Secrets Act," said Leamas, now quite enthusiastically drunk. "Remember how Control used to cheer us on: Tinker, tailor, soldier, spy, let's give it one more Cambridge try!"

I sensed that Leamas' drunkenness was now a source of embarrassment to my other host, so I prepared to take my leave. We shook hands all around. Leamas was barely ambulatory and looked as if he were about to pass out. I thanked them both for their hospitality.

I mounted my horse and rode away, hoping to rejoin my group. I realized that what I had heard at teatime would require much pondering. It would be very trying. Indeed, I began to long for a simpler time when cipher was easy to break and gentlemen, in any case, did not read each other's mail.

The Sisterhood

The classical piece of investigative reporting which revealed the nine Justices of the Supreme Court for the mere mortals they were, was all right in its day, but that work has been superseded by the course of history. Today, as everyone knows, there are no men on the Supreme Court, only women. This transformation is the result of a series of pledges by Presidents to appoint a woman to the highest bench. It is also a reaction to that first series of revelations about the pettiness of the male Justices. Indeed, those revelations were seized upon by certain reactionary elements to settle old scores with the Supreme Court, dating back to the tenure of Earl Warren as Chief Justice. "As long as those guys are going to be so bitchy," said one persistent senatorial critic of the Court, "who cares if the Justices are all women? That's what they should be."

One needn't accept this stark assessment in order to realize that an exposé of the current, all-female Supreme Court is long overdue. This has not been easy to come by. Women may be stigmatized as gossips, but they do have a way of keeping their own secrets. Certainly, only the most reckless journalists would tangle with the current crew.

Nonetheless, it has been possible to piece together a coherent account of the condition of the contemporary Court. Indeed, a mélange (or is it a collage?) of diaries, purloined letters, draft opinions, scraps of half-written verse, and small pieces of marble chipped from the building's exterior tells a story of its own. What it reveals, in plain fact, is the story of an institution in transition, or if not in transition at least in mid-life crisis. But perhaps, overall, this judgment is too severe.

We must begin with capsule biographies of the current members of the Court, the Court which struck down the opinion of Freud that anatomy is destiny and enshrined, instead, the older literary maxim that biography is destiny (or is it that history is biography?). For simplicity, analysts of the Court now call it the Magruder Court, after the sitting Chief Justice, Marjorie Magruder, or Mother Marge, as the other Justices refer to her behind her back, or Big Mama Mag, as they sometimes refer to her on other occasions. Mama Margie, at age seventy-four, has not slowed down a bit. She was never a modern feminist, of course, and she is still regarded as an Aunt Tabby by most of her sisters. They resent the fact that Big Mama flirts outrageously with the reporters who cover the Court's oral arguments. Worse, they resent her penchant for being too cute. After all, it was Mother Marge who voted on both sides of a controversial 5–4 decision, so that the Court overturned its previous ruling. And she had done this without issuing a written opinion in either instance. Instead, she dismissed all questions with a flap of the hand, and a response in her Tennessee drawl: "Sugar, a woman got a right to change her mind, now don't she?" The whole episode was an embarrassment to the women's movement.

Second in influence to the Chief is, of course, Carmelita Estabana. Justice Estabana is the first non-American ever to sit on the Supreme Court. In fact, at the time of her appointment, she spoke no English whatsoever. She was appointed in response to agitation among Hispanic-Americans for the appointment of a Hispanic, a *real* Hispanic, and not some warmed-over Hispanic-American, to the Court. Justice Estabana was, at that time, the most distinguished jurist in Guatemala, and she was given the position. Being Guatemalan, Justice Estabana knew little of the Anglo-American common law, but this has proved less of a problem than some had feared. Indeed, her opinions refer to rulings of the Iberian courts of the 1580's and the Code Napoléon, thus helping to make our narrow tradition of jurisprudence a bit more cosmopolitan.

Justice Estabana is also responsible for the only interesting innovation in the Court's appearance since powdered wigs were abandoned. The Justices no longer wear boring black robes. Instead they wear colorful ruanas of every size and description. All agree that this is a vast improvement.

The third most influential of the Justices is Priscilla Coldtree of Nutny, Vermont. Justice Coldtree is a stern New Englander, now in her sixty-first year, appointed to fill the Vermont seat on the Court. Justice Coldtree seldom issues written opinions. When she does, they invariably consist of a "no" vote on a petition for *certiorari,* accompanied by the traditional aphorism "If it ain't broke, don't fix it." Justice Coldtree is a hard woman. She once argued that torture is constitutional.

There are six other lady Justices, but no one pays much attention to them because the "word" is that each and every one of them is under the thumb of her husband. Curiously, every one of the husbands in question is a Foreign Service officer whose wife attained her law degree by going to law school at night, after the children were grown or had gone off to boarding school.

These nine women should not be taken as representative of women as such or of Americans as a whole. This is quite obvious after our secret papers are examined. It can now be reported, for example, that furious disagreements have racked the Mama Magruder Court, even as the veneer of civility has been maintained. Obviously, the presence of nine members on the Court means that there can be but two four-handed canasta or bridge games. One of the Justices is always left out in the cold, and must play solitaire. The possibility of three three-handed pinochle games had been raised, but was overruled on the grounds that women don't play pinochle.

But this is only one source of the internal bickering. Another is lunch. Traditionally, the Justices ate together at a long wooden table. But some of them were dieting, and they began to resent the fact that the thinner ones could eat their fill of meat and potatoes while those prone to overweight had to eat nothing but yogurt and drink nothing but tea. This antagonism simmered for a while, until it erupted in a fullfledged food fight in the Justices' Dining Room. Someone went so far as to throw an enchilada at Justice Estabana, which hit her on the cabeza. It pains your reporter to have to reveal this infantile behavior, but journalistic honesty requires it.

When the Justices are not throwing food at each other, they will sometimes play croquet on the lawn. There are also enough of them to field one baseball team, but there is no one to play against, because no one else is in their league. Six of the Justices drive to their chambers every day, two use mopeds, and one takes the bus. However, on rainy days, the two who use mopeds will either take taxis or ask their husbands for a lift. This has never been revealed before.

Sometimes, when there is spare time, the Justices will all gather in the Justices' Screening Room and see a new first-run film. They see only G-rated movies, so as to set a good example. Sometimes, they bicker endlessly about which movie they will see. Sometimes, the bickering becomes so heated that the projectionist in the Screening Room will storm out in a huff, screaming obscenities. We have interviewed this projectionist. He said it was simpler to run the Justices' Screening Room when all the Justices were men because all they wanted to see were old Clint Eastwood movies. This is why *that* Court always supported capital punishment, or so the projectionist believes.

Another revelation, bound to sour Americans on this institution, concerns the events of last December when the Justices decided to go on a ski trip. They went by chartered bus to Spindletop and spent the day skiing. Justice Stephanie Speakton broke her right ankle while skiing. This caused her to vote with the plaintiff in the famous case of *Skier* v. *Mountainside*, which claimed that skiing was unconstitutional. Justice Speakton should have recused herself, since she had a personal grudge against skiing, but she didn't. Now that this has been revealed, it is a scandal.

The reader may be shocked by these disclosures but, all in all, these new facts hardly end the argument about whether men are superior to women, or vice versa. As best one can figure it out, the Sisterhood gets along more or less as well as the Brethren. Whether the behavior of both groups can be termed childish is something which must be left to empirical observation, for sooner or later the Supreme Court will consist of nothing but nine minors. This is the way of the world.

Meanwhile, there have been some improvements. After the rash of food fights which erupted in the Justices' Dining Room, the dining room was closed and the Justices took to bringing sandwiches from home or sending out for tacos. However, well-placed informants inside the Supreme Court Building report that the dining room has been reopened, that luncheon is being served, and that no rolls have been thrown for several months. This is to be welcomed. As one of the Sisterhood has said, "Good lunches make good law."

Politics on Tap

The distillation of alcoholic spirit is the oldest-regulated industry in America, the one with the most burden-some system of taxation, the one most prone to fuel anti-government, anti-taxation ferment. This has been true since the time of Shays's Rebellion, in 1786. Thus, bars of all sorts are an engine of social discontent. They were the first places where rapid increases in the price of imported beer came to be seen as a function of the dollar's international difficulties. They became the sites of furious discussions over the respective merits of price controls, devaluation, return to the gold standard, abolition of environmental standards, and the like. In fact, what we now think of as "the new economics" was actually invented in Captain Henry's, a small bar where the customers first noted the demand inelasticity of Heineken beer. The consumption of Heineken continued to increase, *despite* progressive increases in the value of the Dutch guilder as against the American dollar—a result exactly the opposite of what traditional economics would have predicted! As Tim Meinhoff, the former barman in Captain Henry's, put it, "It is one thing to close the gold window, and another to open a beer keg.

"Yeah," he continued, "man is what he eats—as the German fella once put it—or at least what he drinks. Ya can spout theories till you're blue in the face, but that won't help your domestic breweries none. Next thing ya know they want import controls, higher tariffs, non-tariff barriers. I tried to tell my customers that such intrusions into the free market process would wreak havoc with the theory of comparative advantage. But did they care? Nah, all they tell me is 'Shut up and pour.' So I pour. Hell, I'm an economic animal, even if they're not. So that's why I had to leave Captain Henry's and open up my own place, ya understand. It just happens that the purveying of alcoholic beverages by the drink, retail, is a business with a low cost of entry—basically, all ya need is the bribe to get the license, if ya know what I mean. And I've been doin' O.K. these past few years since I hung out my own sign.

"I'll tell ya something," said Meinhoff. "Used to be people wanted a neighborhood tavern they could come to and talk about baseball or complain about the old lady. That's the kind of place my old man ran. Now they want a place where they can come talk about economics, public policy, marginal tax rates, whether birth control is good for boy-girl relationships, stuff like that.

"Now, ya ask me where I got the idea for that new place of mine. I'll tell ya. People would come in and tell me that all they could talk about in bars these days was socialism and women's liberation. If ya went to one of those places and ya had a beef about the money supply, nobody would give ya the time of day. So I figured, hell, here's some demand, and I'll be the supply, so to speak."

Money was not all that tight in the mid-1960's, and Meinhoff was able to raise what he needed to open his own establishment in Washington, not far from the White House, which he called Master Ludwig's. After a while, it became the place to go if you were of a certain sort. "It requires a change in attitude, if ya know what I mean," said Meinhoff. "I mean, I used to be a typical barkeeper. A guy would come in, he'd have a couple of drinks, he'd tell me how his girlfriend had two-timed him, and I would agree that was in the nature of women to behave like that, and then maybe he'd have a hamburger and one for the road and that would be it. Now it's a different kind of thing. Of course, it took a little getting used to. A guy comes in, he has a couple of drinks, he tells me that the money supply is increasing too rapidly, and I say, yeah, that's right, it's in the nature of the Fed to increase the money supply too rapidly, and he would say I was the first barkeeper he ever met who understood anything. Then he buys another couple of drinks, and then he starts bringing over a bunch of his friends, and I don't know much about the Fed's money supply, except that I notice that my own money supply is increasing, so why should I complain? It's like my father always told me: 'Ya wanna be a successful tavern owner, ya gotta be a good listener.'

"But the real success of my new bar," Meinhoff said, "was based on the simple fact that I refused to extend credit. I mean, in the old place, if you didn't take checks or credit cards, or if you wouldn't extend credit, people thought you were unfriendly. In my new place, they love it. They tell me I'm being patriotic. My best customers don't even pay in cash, they pay in gold bullion. They tell me that every time I extend credit, I'm really expanding the money supply. And I say, sure, that's why I don't do it, patriotism and all that. So a guy wants to think I'm patriotic because I won't put anything on the arm, I'm not gonna argue with him."

Meinhoff continued, "I'll tell ya when business really began to boom around this place. One day this guy comes in wearing a lavender leisure suit with a parrot perched on his shoulder, which is not so strange to me because, if you tend bar, you see everything sooner or later. And he begins to explain to me that if the government would just collect lower taxes, it would have more money, which sounds fine to me, because I'm like the next man, and don't like to pay taxes. And everybody thinks this is terrific, so they all start buying him drinks, and pretty soon, I've got a pretty popular Washington spot, because all these congressmen show up to shoot the breeze about taxes. And three months after that, some reporter comes from *Esquire* magazine and tells me I have now become the bartender to the neoconservative movement, and what do I think about that? So I tell him I think that's just fine, because a dollar's a dollar, no matter how ya earn it, as long as it's legal, if ya know what I mean."

It was only much later that anyone noticed that Master Ludwig's was thought to have been named after a famous Austrian economist. Meinhoff no longer denies it, though he once admitted it was actually named after his neighbor's German shepherd. "I'm a practical man," Meinhoff told the interviewer from *Esquire*, "and I figured since I had a little extra cash, I might as well open another spot in town, which is also doing all right. I mean, a guy comes into my new place, tells me the oil companies make too much money, which is O.K. by me, because as long as he keeps buying drinks for himself and his friends, I'm not gonna argue with him either. When it comes to tending bar, ya have to be flexible.

"And so whatever happens in the next election, I figure I'll still be able to make a buck, which, after all, is what America is all about. Am I right? Or am I right?"

Star-Crossed Lawyers

For many years, Senator Wimbol had been the sole committee chairman to have engaged the services of a professional astrologer as Special Counselor. It had been the astrologer's mission to provide new insights into what old-fashioned political scientists had called the "legislative process." Extensive research, all of it computerized, had revealed that the most likely predictor of whether any particular bill would be enacted into law was the conjunction of the planets and the arrangement of the constellations on the day a piece of legislation had been introduced. Thus, before Wimbol's committee would even begin to consider any piece of legislation, Madame Blitter, the astrologer, would prepare its chart. This, in turn, would be correlated with the chart of the bill's principal sponsor, the charts of the members of the committee, and, most importantly, the chart of Wimbol himself.

From the beginning, it had been evident that there would

be difficulties in reducing the analysis to coherent committee procedure. In the first place, of the fifteen members of the committee, eleven had been born on a "cusp" between two signs. This accounted for their indecisiveness and ambiguity on important matters of policy. And since the cuspians constituted the majority, the committee seemed forever bogged down in meaningless discussion. Wimbol himself—as were most strong committee chairmen—was an Aries, determined to ram through measures with the least attention to detail and nuance. His counterpart among the minority members was a Taurus, bullheaded and stubborn, inclined toward obstructionism for its own sake. Of the six members of the committee under age fifty, four were born under the sign of Aquarius, given over, in the main, to jolly patter and backslapping, prone to turn each committee drafting session into a celebration of lawmaking as a form of individual expression and creativity. One of them, in fact, was rumored to be a regular user of controlled substances.

In the second place, Madame Blitter's analysis had revealed an unarguable correlation between the special interests of senators on the one hand and the signs of their birth on the other. The pattern was unmistakable. Of nine pieces of legislation concerning gun control and the regulation of firearms generally that had been introduced in the last session, seven had been introduced by senators born under the sign of Sagittarius: as archers, they no doubt were summoned back to a more primitive time when the true symbol of manhood had been the English yeoman and his trusty longbow. Among the eight senators pushing most vigorously for a constitutional amendment outlawing abortion, six had been born under the sign of Virgo, a sure indication that they regarded virginity as the highest condition of womankind, all violations of which ought to be punished and stigmatized. Curiously, this had nothing to do with religious background, for among the six, there were two Catholics, two Mormons, and two Jews. Without doubt, astrological affiliation, not religious confession, was a far better predictor of a senator's position on this burning social question. Most revealing, all nine sponsors of the latest scheme for comprehensive national health insurance had been born under the sign of Cancer. By the same token, not a single tobacco-growing state was represented by a senator born under that ominous sign, a sure indication that the tobacco interests would tolerate not the slightest hint that there was any connection between their product and the dreaded illness.

Stalked by the stars, these and other matters wandered through the Senate's celestial regions.

On those rare occasions when the two principal authors of a bill happened to be a Gemini and a Capricorn respectively, there was no end of trouble. Invariably, the two were improperly mated, their legislative relationship exhilarating at first but fated to dissolve in tempestuous feuding, ending in irreconcilable hostility. Such were the inexorable ways of the heavens. Conversely, Madame Blitter's computerized analysis confirmed what had been expected all along, namely that a joint endeavor involving a Leo and a Pisces made for the smoothest legislative sailing. Here, there was no conflict: the Leo would roar out the requisite rhetoric, the Pisces would be content to meander about the legislative waters, having a soothing effect on the other senators who watched his random comings and goings on the Senate floor. Pisces provoked little hostility from his colleagues, an altogether reassuring and sympathetic figure.

The weight of this data allowed Wimbol to effect the first serious reform of the Senate calendar format in more than a century and a half. Hitherto, bills had been listed thereon by their numerical designation, accompanied by their brief title. Under the "Wimbol Calendar Reform" the bills were also listed by the sign of their date of introduction: thus, one could tell at a glance where each piece of proposed legislation fitted into the great zodiac of lawmaking. Each bill was, furthermore, accompanied by a brief description of its prospects for that particular day, should it be taken off the calendar and placed before the entire Senate for consideration.

Thus, for example, for bills introduced between October 23

and November 21 (Scorpio), the daily legislator's horoscope might warn: "Make sure that promises made to others have been kept; maintain goodwill. Seek passage by further amendment." Or another, this time directed to bills introduced between July 21 and August 22 (Leo), might advise: "Contact many lobbyists who can be helpful with good ideas for bill's passage. Be more accommodating to environmentalists." Or the all-purpose Libra admonition, a sure killer for bills introduced between September 23 and October 22: "Find a better outlet through which to express these public policy purposes. Sidestep those who are doubtful about sponsors' good intentions."

It was only a matter of time before other interested parties desired access to these vague clues to the fate of legislation which could affect their own futures. Trade magazines, political newsletters, and legal journals soon began to print "Madame Blitter's Astrological Guide to Legislative Happenings" on a daily basis, and it was then picked up by newspapers around the country.

The House of Representatives established a similar procedure, thereby ensuring that the two great spheres of lawmaking would, at the least, be seen to be inhabiting the same cosmos. And, not to be outdone by the Senate, the House went even one step beyond. It engaged the services of a psychic who claimed the ability to communicate directly with departed congressmen who had passed to the other side. This was the final triumph of the seniority system, for not even death was able to diminish the influence of the elders on the course of legislative history.

A Convention Carol

"Manolo, before you leave, could you see that the thermostat on the air conditioning is down as far as it can go.
And would you throw another log on the fire?"

"Yes, Mr. President. And is there anything else you would
like?"

"No, there's plenty of hot water left in the kettle, and I'll be
able to fix my own cocoa."

"Very good, Mr. President. Good night—and a Merry Convention to you, sir!"

"Thank you, Manolo."

A Merry Convention, indeed. Humbug. But I suppose I
might as well watch it to the end. Hmmm, it's already past
prime time in the East and it's getting late here too. But I've
got to remember all the details. Who knows? The Chinese
may want to ask me about it. In 1972, they wanted to know
whether Senator Hiram Fong of Hawaii might be on the

ticket, and I told them that Fong didn't have a Chinaman's chance. It must have lost something in the translation. Anyway, what do you tell the Chinese when they ask about court-ordered forced busing? Boy, this thing is really dragging; they could use a Haldeman to move it along.

"Richard, Richard Nixon!"

"Who's that calling me? Who is it?"

"Why, Richard, don't you know me? I am the ghost of Convention Past."

"That's impossible. Anyone will tell you that *I* am the ghost of Convention Past. Oh, well, come a little closer so I can see you."

"Do you recognize me now?"

"Why, it's Everett Dirksen, of Ev and Charlie! Of course I remember you. Gee, Ev, I haven't seen you in a month of Sundays. How have you been? Come over here and sit down; have some cocoa, and watch the convention. See? You can watch all three networks at once. The set was a gift from Prime Minister Tanaka."

"This is very gracious of you, Mr. President. I must say you're looking quite well. I've been dead a few years now and I know how it feels. But I haven't lost my interest in politics, no sir! Of course you know Senator Baker; he's my son-in-law."

"Tiny Howard? How could I forget Tiny Howard?"

"Now, now, that's not being very nice."

"Not nice? Humbug! Didn't you hear that keynote speech of his back in 1976? He referred to me as a set of old bones rattling around in a closet. That's some way to talk about me. Listen, Ev, I made him what he is today. In fact, I made all of them. Where would they be if it hadn't been for me?"

"I suppose that's right. But don't you worry, Mr. President, they'll acknowledge their debt to you as soon as the time is ripe. This isn't Russia, you know. Sooner or later you'll be rehabilitated."

"Fat chance. Anyway, Ev, I'm glad you dropped by to keep

me company. They really are dragging this thing out, and it's good to have someone to talk to. Back in '72 . . ."

"Richard, Richard Nixon!"

"Now who is it?"

"Don't you know me? *I* am the ghost of Convention Past."

"That's ridiculous! If you've watched TV for even five minutes this week, you know that *I* am the ghost of Convention Past. But it doesn't matter. Come on in and join us, whoever you are. But please keep it down; the children are asleep upstairs. And for God's sake, forget that you ever came here. If the Washington *Post* hears that I've been sitting around talking to two old ghosts they'll have a field day!"

"Don't you recognize me, Richard?"

"Step into the light a little more. Well, I'll be! Of course I recognize you! Nelson, how have you been? Say, I thought you were still dead."

"Oh, only in a manner of speaking. I figured I could slip away from that great convention floor in the sky for a few hours and come out and visit you. I'm sure I won't be missed."

"Well, sit down, have a cup of cocoa, and watch the convention. You do remember Ev Dirksen, don't you?"

"Ev, of Ev and Charlie? Of course I remember. How could I forget? Hi ya, fella!"

"Good to see you, Mr. Vice-President. I guess it has been a few years. Dick and I were just reminiscing about the old days. By the way, would you like a copy of one of my records?"

"I've got a complete set, Ev. They're terrific!"

"Ev and Rocky, I can't tell you how good it is to see you. I'm glad you're here. This convention really is something of a bore, isn't it? Now it's almost past prime time in California. According to my watch, it's almost tomorrow morning in Peking."

"Richard, Richard Nixon!"

"Not again! No, don't tell me, let me guess. You're William Miller."

"No, no, no. I am the ghost of Convention *Future!*"

"Well, come out from behind the chair so we can have a good look at you. Upon my word, it's Tiny Howard!"

"A Merry Convention to you, sir. God save you!"

"Humbug. Humbug."

"Convention a humbug, sir? Surely you don't mean that."

"Bah! What is convention good for? Just a lot of noise and commotion. I've always hated them, even the three where I was nominated."

"Tiny Howard, my dear son-in-law! What brings you out here? You should be back in Detroit campaigning for a spot on the ticket!"

"I'm starting to organize for 1984. This candidate doesn't have a chance. Come November 3, everyone will be thinking about 1984 and, by November 4, I'll be the front runner. You can count on it."

"Just like I figured it out in '64! Tiny Howard, how you've grown in my estimation. You're a man after my own heart. I see now that I shouldn't hold your service on the Watergate Committee against you. We all have to get started somewhere. Now, because Ev is such a dear old friend of mine, I insist that you drop the formality and call me Uncle Dick."

"That's very big of you, Mr. President. As for that business about the old bones rattling in the closet, well, I really didn't mean anything by it."

"Tiny Howard, you are a devoted son-in-law, coming all the way here to see me. You're one of the boys, yes sir! You know, even Rocky and I would get carried away now and then. Why, when I said those things about Dewey back in '52, people thought I was being vindictive. That reminds me; Dewey hasn't spoken to me since. I must look him up and set things straight. And back in '76, I'm sure you saw Rocky embrace Barry right there in Walter Cronkite's anchor booth, so we know that Rocky is still a large man."

"One of the largest, fella!"

"Gee, a guy like me, just starting out, getting to spend convention night with all you elder statesmen. They'll never believe this in Nashville. Mr. President, thank you for bringing us all together."

"Yes, it is wonderful to have all of you with me this convention night. O.K., I see the roll call is finally going to start—so may the best man win.

"And God bless us all, each and every one."

Washington Whirlaround

Highly placed, ultra-confidential sources yield shocking reports of the latest threats to privacy in America. Caught out by the rapid proliferation of miniaturized psychological stress evaluators which, unbeknownst to a speaker, can detect falsehoods in human speech by measuring minute changes in the voice pattern, government scientists are hard at work on a new machine which will give them a leg up in hunting out private prevarication. Designed as an attachment to the standard office copying machine—whether Xerox, IBM, or Toshiba—the device will immediately detect any lies which appear on the printed or written page. Preliminary tests show the device's capability, even when scanning a chart of statistics! Six arithmetical errors were found in the President's fiscal year 1981 budget submission.

Powerful insiders in the journalistic community have held a

series of hush-hush meetings, hoping to organize a campaign to destroy the machine and its blueprints and drawings. What is feared is that every home in America will soon be equipped to scan the stories in the morning news. Scientists attached to the White House Press Office are already experimenting with the machinery as a way of intimidating errant journalists. "They thought they would drive us out of office as soon as they tuned in on the President with those psychological stress evaluators," one top White House aide was heard to chortle, "but we've got those bastards now! We ran the latest issue of *Newsweek* through the system, and that goddamn machine damn near blew its damnself damnup!"

Ominous, startling, a threat to the future of the printed page in America. Thoughtful constitutional lawyers are already arguing among themselves whether the machinery is a threat to fundamental First Amendment protections. "There is nothing less at stake here," said Harrison R. Harrison, legal counsel to Time, Inc., "than the public's right not merely not to know, but to remain unsure. All this has grievous overtones for the sanctity of the editorial process."

As far as this corner is concerned, Harrison is right on the money. There's a big story brewing here, and we are going to get it, even if we have to run a smiling picture of Jody Powell through our Xerox to find out what he's really thinking.

Government officials and harried legislators, long wallowing in a mountain of paper, have been flocking to speed-reading courses in order to wade through their daily business more efficiently. Now educational science comes to their aid once again, with the opening of Marvin Eardo's Institute of Hearing Dynamics. Eardo is the originator of the revolutionary technique of speed hearing, which allows the hearer to hear at no less than four times the normal rate.

Speed hearing, so Eardo's brochure explains, is a genuine time saver. It allows a busy senator to get through the usual thirty-minute nightly news program in only seven and a half minutes. Likewise, it takes but fifteen minutes to hear all of a customary one-hour briefing at the Department of Agriculture. It should be pointed out that speed hearing has nothing whatever to do with speed speaking, since the system does not rely on the speaker's speaking any faster than usual. In fact, it doesn't matter whether he speaks slower than usual. Embarrassing stammers and stutters, ahems and uhs, phrases like "the nit of it is . . ." or "the bottom line," no matter how frequently introduced, will not affect the hearer's hearing speed, once he is properly trained.

The rush to speed-hearing courses is now well under way. We can report to our readers in the hinterland that the courses are what explain the mass departures from the House Chamber during the President's most recent State of the Union address. It was not a walkout with any political connotations. Rather, most of the audience was able to hear all of the President's ninety-minute talk in about twenty-two and a half minutes, and therefore had no reason to stay any longer. And, as Dr. Eardo has pointed out, if the President had reduced his speech to a mere forty minutes, those who had mastered the speed-hearing technique would have been long gone in no more than twelve minutes, thirteen at the most. This also explains the newfound tendency of telephone calls in the Nation's Capital to end abruptly as listeners suddenly hang up even though the caller thinks he has only covered a quarter of the points he had intended to bring up.

The secret to the technique, apparently, is the use of the eyelid as a pacer. As the speaker speaks, the listener's eyelids are supposed to blink at an ever faster rate, thereby speeding up the hearing process. The advanced course combines the advantages of rapidly blinking eyelids with training in rapid lateral eye movement.

Cosmetic surgery is becoming more and more of a godsend to aging politicians. No fewer than sixteen prominent political personalities and their wives are reported to have had face-lifts in the past four months, and this does not include work done on their children to correct defects of face and form.

But the obvious trend toward the election of younger people to office has the Capital's cosmetic surgeons a bit worried.

Actuarial analysis shows that for the next twenty years or so there will be a rapid drop-off in the requirement for face-lift, with a rapid rise after 1999. Accordingly, in order to even out this expected curve, the Board of Cosmetic Surgery has undertaken a new campaign, and meeting with substantial success, to bring the benefits of cosmetic surgery to the young, when they really need it but don't realize that they need it.

The key to it all is the new surgical technique of face-lowering. More and more political figures are beginning to understand the advantages of having their faces lowered at the beginning of their political careers rather than having their faces lifted when they are near the end of it. In fact, it is this new face-lowering procedure which gives the appearance that the aging process has been retarded, not the other way around as once had been believed. Indeed, the ravages of the decades can be compressed into a single four-hour operation, and an aspiring politician need no longer worry about the problem. Thus, one thirty-two-year-old congressman acquired the face of a man in his late fifties. His colleagues did remark that he seemed a bit tired, but they attributed this to an extended debate on a bill establishing a new Department of Instrumentation. But then they began to notice, as the years wore on, that he appeared to be getting no older at all, and he soon acquired a reputation for remarkable vigor and fitness, even though he had a dangerously high cholesterol level.

Sociologists, media consultants, and advertising agencies would be well advised to begin studying the implications of this social revolution, for all politicians, without exception, will appear to be exactly the same age—fifty-four—no matter whether lifted or lowered into that appearance. This, we suspect, is what lies behind the President's adoption of a new hairdo. But sooner or later, the truth will come out. Our team of investigative reporters has tracked down the leading plastic surgeon of Americus, Georgia, who seems to have a recollection that back in 1974 or thereabouts he lowered the face of a rather bright teen-ager from a nearby town.

Wimbol for President

Senator Wimbol was a driven man. Even though he was now one hundred and forty-six years old, he was still driven. One can imagine his mental state by noting this simple fact: he had served in the Senate for almost one hundred and fourteen years and had never been elected President of the United States. Indeed, he had never received the Presidential nomination of any party at any time for the nation's highest office. He had seen men of far less ability, some not even a third his age, ascend to the Chief Magistracy, while he himself remained a veritable prisoner in the Capitol.

It was not for lack of trying. For Wimbol had sought the Presidency many times. He had pursued delegates in every corner of the United States. He had run in primaries, secondaries, and tertiaries. He had been listed on straw polls, hay polls, alfalfa polls, and polls made of hops, rice, barley, and the finest of malt. (He had once won a flax poll in South Carolina.) He had campaigned in conventions and caucuses. He once traveled to Russia to address a caucus of expatriates living in the Caucasus. He had eaten breakfast, brunch, lunch, dinner, and midnight supper with prospective delegates. He had tasted every form of cuisine. He had been to coffees and teas for normal people, and to Sankas and Postums for insomniacs. At one time or another, he had employed at least one member of every ethnic group listed in the *Times World Atlas*. He had published campaign literature in seventy-one languages. He had ridden in every manner of conveyance—on land, above and below the sea, and in the air. He had campaigned in deep-diving submersibles and hydrogen-filled zeppelins. He had appeared in every type of spot—radio spots, television spots, video cassette spots to be played in the privacy of the voter's bedroom. He had recorded his speeches on long-playing record albums; he had starred in movies about himself. He had appeared on the cover of no fewer than forty-one well-known magazines. He had undergone religious conversion, deconversion, and reconversion.

He had also employed directors. He had an issues director, an advertising director, a mailing director, a media director, an agricultural director, a horticultural director, and a countercultural director. He had a movie director, a television director, and a traffic director. He also had many telephone directories—one for every city and town in the United States. He had an entourage which included bright young men, wise old men, and anxious middle-aged men, and which also included liberated women, unliberated women, and little children. Over the years, he had also compiled a record, which could be looked at. The record consisted of positions he had taken, including all of the positions in the *Kamasutra*. He had spoken candidly, forthrightly, honestly, frankly, truthfully, sincerely, credibly, forcefully, and convincingly. He had been dismayed, shocked, outraged, and appalled. He had believed in the people of America, and also in its trees.

On every occasion when he had done all of these things, Wimbol had deserved to win, for his opponents had never done any of them. Nor did it matter from whence Wimbol had started. He had been in his time the front runner, the back runner, the side runner, the up runner and the down runner. He had walked on the down side, and had been the first politician in America ever to cross the bottom line. It was a turning point in American history, and his crossing of the bottom line was broadcast on national television.

Thus, even in his one hundred and forty-sixth year, the thought of running came once again into Wimbol's mind.

Now, this process of running had changed from what it once was. In the main, the pursuit of the Presidency had become an occupation for men otherwise unemployed. Indeed, it was the ultimate expression of the theory of unemployment compensation, for the federal fisc offered subsidy to those who undertook it. It was true, of course, that one could hold a job and also run for the Presidency; some incumbents had done that. But for Wimbol, who always had his eye on the future, another run for the Presidency seemed a not uninteresting way to retire in style.

He consulted with his lawyers, accountants, and actuaries. They devised for him a retirement program in the form of a Presidential Campaign Annuity. One need only raise a small sum of money from supportive donors, qualify for federal matching funds, convert the funds into certificates of deposit and use the proceeds to finance what would be, in effect, a perpetual, revolving-charge Presidential campaign. The main advantage of this scheme would be apparent in the wintertime, when trips to Florida and to Palm Springs could be financed on the grounds that the Senator was a candidate campaigning for the imminent caucus, since a caucus would always be imminent. If it were alleged that Wimbol was doing nothing but vacationing at the contributors' expense, his media director and his issues director advised him to respond that he was pursuing a southern strategy.

As the cold weather approached, Wimbol felt constrained to implement this scheme. He contracted for a Caribbean cruise, scheduled to stop at all the romantic West Indian ports of call. It was hailed in the press as a case of innovative campaigning, for, as the Senator pointed out, his cruise mates were indeed Americans, and his own purpose in going was to work the captain's dinner table at dinnertime, at both the first and second sittings. So far as the ports were concerned, they too were throbbing with throngs of Americans, always ready to interrupt their shopping sprees to shake the hand of a declared candidate. Moreover, they vowed to support Wimbol when next they attended their local caucus.

Wimbol applied the same technique to his visits to golf courses in southern Florida. One invariably came upon a threesome anxious to become a foursome and, as Wimbol pointed out, there was nothing like the long walk from tee to green to win over three previously uncommitted golfers. As everyone knows, this tactic was the basis for the famous Hole Poll, the informal, though rigorously scientific sampling of golfers after they had left the eighteenth green bound for the clubhouse. And the process could always be reversed as the campaign season heated up in the summertime. While others worked the teeming cities, Wimbol worked the northern New England seacoast. As convention time drew near, Wimbol would be off searching for elusive uncommitted delegates on the active ski slopes of the Southern Hemisphere.

No one knows exactly how the new practices of campaigning produced the revolutionary developments in the nominating process we have now come to observe, but clearly there is a connection. After all, no one was especially surprised when, at the most recent nominating convention, two states had simply refused to be represented. They had announced beforehand that they would not be sending delegates—first, because they didn't feel like it and, second, because they couldn't see any purpose to it. At first the National Committee had thought this a ploy. Representatives were dispatched to the offending states in a vain effort to strike a deal. "We'll go on without you if you refuse to come," the National Committeemen had threatened. "Fine with us," said the insurgents, "we'd just as soon stay home and watch it on television."

The absent delegates came in for a fair amount of abuse, but as the nominating convention droned on into its forty-fifth ballot, the wisdom of non-attendance became more apparent. Hot and sweaty delegates prowled the arena. When they had agreed to set the arena's thermostat at eighty-one degrees in order to conserve energy, they had not realized that the convention would drag on for many days. "Why are we going through this," one of them began to complain, "just so *they* can have a Presidential candidate? They're only going to bitch about the outcome, and may not even end up supporting the nominee of the party." "Absolutely right," chimed in another. "Why can't we sit in air-conditioned comfort and have somebody go through this tedious business for us?"

This manner of grumbling soon became widespread. Gradually, the delegates began to leave for home. In two days, only fourteen delegates were left, far short of the 1,319 needed for nomination. To the embarrassment of the National Committee, the convention was obliged to adjourn *sine die* without nominating anybody, the first time in anyone's memory that this had happened. Not even Wimbol could recall a similar event.

And so it happened that, for the first time, the Party lost the Presidential election by default. Four years later, the same trend manifested itself in the Other Party. The Incumbent, thinking himself assured of renomination, arrived in the arena only to note that the cavernous room held but thirty-one people, all with their noses buried in a book of convention rules. This, too, was far short of the magic number needed to nominate. Political pundits were puzzled. For years, they had complained about the proliferation of Presidential candidates. Now, in less than half a decade, the country had reached a condition where neither party had nominated a Presidential candidate, with the result that no one ran for the office. Hence, there was no campaign to analyze.

There was a genuine need for Reform. Naturally, the first solution proposed was a reduction in the magic number needed to nominate to about thirteen or so. This would more than compensate for any "no shows" at future conventions. Others thought this too inflexible. Finally, it was decided to leave the business to whoever managed to show up. And yet, it was soon realized that it was television which was holding down attendance. As the Commissioner had pointed out, television had ruined the movie business and was on the verge of ruining professional sports. The obvious answer was a television blackout, so that the convention could not be seen in its Home Town. "We can't sell tickets if people know they are able to sit home and watch our game on television," the Commissioner had testified before several congressional committees. Everyone knew that pay TV was out of the question, for it seemed inconceivable that anyone would pay to see the game at home.

Accordingly, both National Committees adopted a policy of totally blacking out convention proceedings. Now, no one has any idea what transpires at such gatherings, even though attendance at them has increased—though it is not yet anywhere near previous levels.

As for Wimbol, out on the campaign trail once again, the new system has produced anxiety and uncertainty. After all, a couple of hundred people gathered in a gleaming Convention Hall might, through some fluke, actually nominate him, thereby ending whatever chance he had for a comfortable retirement. But then, as he concluded, it wouldn't much matter, because nobody would know about it.

Haiku on the Issues

(It had begun as an "outreach" campaign of the traditional sort, an effort to ensure that the diverse ethnic groups of America would be properly involved in the political process. It culminated in a pamphlet published by the Committee to Elect the Candidate, targeted for Japanese-Americans. "Brevity is the soul of Japanese," the counselor on Japanese affairs had said, "so keep it simple. No more than seventeen syllables, one haiku, our traditional verse form. Five syllables, then seven syllables, then five more, and that's all. If you can't say it in seventeen syllables, you can't say it at all!" Nor, he added, does this approach tax the attention span. The pamphlet was a remarkable success.)

The Tax Revolt
Skyward taxes fly.
Polls Float on Fickle Feelings.
We tack to the Right.

On the Successful Outcome of Mideast Negotiations
Arab and Jew met.
Semites spoke English, thank God;
Peace came just in time.

The Strategic Nuclear Balance of Forces
One Rocket goes up.
Twenty-four warheads come down.
We head for the Hills.

The Sino-Soviet Rift
Words from Mao: "Dig deep,
Store rice, tell Brezhnev, 'Your mom
Wears big army boots!'"

The Political Significance of the Panama Canal
Straw hats with wide bands,
We have not heard the last from
Omar Torrijos.

Where Do Correct Political Ideas Come From?
We don't smoke but we
Love our coke. Sweet treat. Cocaine,
Runnin' round our brain.

Immigrants
Mex treks sure scare Tex!
Red as unpicked tomatoes,
López Portillo.

The Free Enterprise System
Deregulation.
Smash greedy airline cartel.
All dig cheap airfare.

Co-opted by the System
Scuffed boots on the shelf.
Now he wears a pin-striped suit.
Hamilton Jordan.

The Legacy of John Maynard Keynes
Tax tax tax tax tax
Spend spend spend spend spend spend spend
Elect elect el-

The Religious Issue
Buddhism's passé,
And yoga's not the way to
One-up Jerry Brown.

Fear and Loathing on the Campaign Trail
Election Day comes,
Surly electorate waves
"Sayonara."

The Commanding Heights

I took my genuine seal-hide, Eskimo, handmade kayak out into the middle of the Potomac River for my daily paddling exercise. I headed upstream, minding my own business, and reached the point where the high ground above the river provided pleasing views to those who lived there. These were old Washingtonians indeed, long unaffected by the vicissitudes of life in the downtown Washington lowlands.

I had gone not another quarter of a mile when I found myself surrounded by six canoes, each carrying a group of six paddlers, equally divided between men and women. They appeared hostile. Their canoes were made of genuine birch bark. Men and women alike wore red chamois shirts, denim pants, and well-wrought leather boots, all of the finest quality.

"You ought to know," one of them said, "that we are the maritime arm of the Palisades Liberation Organization."

"Surely, not *the* PLO, of which I have heard so much," I answered.

"The same," he said.

"Well," I answered, "I really ought not to be seen speaking with you. Otherwise, I'll find myself in a kettle of hot water at the Bureau of Recreation of the Department of the Interior, where I work. The Department of the Interior doesn't recognize you, and that's that." And, having clearly enunciated Department policy, I began to execute a reverse J stroke, so as to turn about, and end the discussion.

"We'd rather parlay in a relaxed manner," said the man from the PLO, "and I hope we do not have to hijack you in broad daylight in order to get you to listen to our just case."

"Why pick on me?" I asked. "I mean, the Secretary of the Interior and the Director of the National Park Service are both seriously into sculling. One of them is bound to come along here sooner or later, and then you can present your case at the highest level."

"The heroic struggle of the Palisadian people to secure autonomy over their native high ground will certainly be vindicated by the movement of history," replied the man from the PLO. "Palisadia is ours, and we are not about to turn it over to real estate developers and others who will brutally exploit us and end up expropriating our birthright through clever speculations in land and houses."

"I know," I said, "that the Palisadians are a great people who have, for two centuries, struggled against attempts at oppression which originate in the lowlands of downtown Washington, D.C." And, as I said that, I recalled the daring raid the Palisadians had staged last year, when they kidnapped the president of Washington's largest real estate firm, and held him captive for sixty-one days, until all their demands had been met.

"Sooner or later," said the man from the PLO, "you lowlanders are going to have to negotiate with us directly. No more middlemen; no more dummy corporations; no more enticing advertisements in the daily press. Palisadia must become an autonomous, self-governing region of the District of Columbia, or there will be no peace in these regions."

I was much taken by the forcefulness with which the PLO spokesman had articulated the PLO's long-standing demand. I didn't know many of the details, but from time to time, in my capacity at the Department of the Interior, I had to deal with complaints from innocent boaters and hikers that they had been fired upon from the top of the Potomac Palisades whenever they ventured too far north on the river. Naturally, the Palisadians would not cooperate with the federal authorities, and all investigations into these incidents had come to a dead end.

Both the local authorities and the Department of the Interior had been admonished to tread gingerly into this controversy. Both were bound by the provisions of City Council Resolution 242, a two-part document which affirmed Palisadian rights on the one hand, but recognized only their duly elected City Councilperson as their authorized representative on the other. So even as I floated on the river, I knew I was in the midst of a political thicket.

There was an ominous tone in the voice of the PLO spokesman as he resumed our conversation. "You have been selected," he said, "to carry back to the lowlanders a message of the utmost gravity. Unless our demands for autonomy are fully met, we will close the river to further pleasure-boat traffic. Moreover, we have reached the breaking point so far as the noise of low-flying aircraft, bound for Washington National Airport, is concerned. We have procured a supply of hand-held antiaircraft weapons, and six days from now we will open fire on all airplanes which violate our sacred airspace. The city will be cut off from the rest of the world, and will be accessible only by unreliable rail service."

Now, here was a threat worth taking seriously. The Palisades were the strategic key to control of the District of Columbia. If they were to fall under the control of forces implacably hostile to the purposes of the Federal City, a crisis of grave proportions would ensue. No tactic, however uncivilized, was beyond these dangerous madmen. Even as we talked, I could imagine that a battalion of Cuban soldiers was

secretly training guerrilla fighters, and that our very meeting was being observed by North Korean pilots flying aerial reconnaissance missions. My blood froze.

"Your approach to these issues is really quite un-American," I volunteered, a note of reproach creeping into my voice. "After all, we all purchase our outdoor gear from the same mail-order supply house in New England, and this ought to establish some common ground between us. No one will win from the senseless escalation of this dispute."

"We demand the appointment of a Special Envoy," the Palisadian said, "without any ifs, ands, or buts. We demand the right to fly our own flag, and we demand that the birthday of our founder be declared a national holiday, to be celebrated, without fail, the third day of each November."

I was temporarily startled by this last demand, for I knew little of the history of the Palisades Liberation Organization, and had never even heard of its founder. Not wishing to offer offense, I stalled for time.

"Your founder," I said, "of course, your founder. A concerned citizen."

"Very much so," replied the Palisadian. "Fireside Whetstone—his actual name, though often called Whetstone Fireside by some confused by the fact that he seemed to have two last names—was the man who molded our inchoate discontents into a formidable armed struggle. He, of course, was the gentlest of men, and a terrible public speaker, an incurable mumbler in fact."

"What was his original line of work?" I asked.

"He was a Foreign Service officer of Class 2," said the Palisadian, "and was for twenty-seven years the official Deputy Media Liaison Spokesperson at the Department of State. He was admirably situated to observe the best way to get a hearing for one's grievances. After observing the responses of the Department of State to developments on the international scene, he concluded that the Department of the Interior would respond in similar fashion to similar tactics. This was a great insight."

"How did he do it?" I asked.

"Mr. Whetstone was the first member of our ineffectual moribund citizens association to suggest that we shave only every third day, and that we wear dark sunglasses, even at nighttime. If we did that, he argued, everyone would think that we were pretty tough. Then he drafted a Covenant of Palisadian Rights for us, our Declaration of Independence he called it. All groups like ours need a covenant, so that it can be called our Declaration of Independence. Likewise, all countries need a George Washington. This was another profound insight of Mr. Whetstone's. George Washington is the George Washington of the United States. Yasir Arafat is the George Washington of Palestine. Fireside Whetstone is the George Washington of Palisadia. Everybody who's anybody anywhere in the world these days is the George Washington of some place or other." At this point, he withdrew a long list from his shirt pocket and began reading off the names of prominent world figures in alphabetical order, beginning with Amin and ending with Somoza.

With the notion that Anastasio Somoza (the elder) had been the George Washington of Nicaragua still spinning in my head, I noticed that he had replaced the list. He commented, "So you see, as Mr. Whetstone pointed out to anyone who would listen, the Palisadian Liberation Organization is as American as apple pie. We are up in the mountains, our oppressors are down in the plains. We work by day and fight by night, whereas with you lowlanders it is just the other way around. We shave every third day, you shave every day. That's the nub of it."

I couldn't quarrel with what he had said. I myself had always identified with the liberation forces, wherever they might happen to be. What concerned American could not?

"There is much to what you say," I acknowledged, "but I must tell you that the Interior Department and the State Department are not cut from the same cloth. My own superiors are a crusty bunch. They all own rifles and many of them are secret members of the National Rifle Association. But I don't know of anyone at the State Department who would get near a firearm, let alone actually own one. No, sir; they're not much for sensible compromise at the Interior Department."

"That doesn't much surprise me," said the Palisadian, who cleaned his sunglasses with a handkerchief as he spoke. "Mr. Whetstone told us it might take years, decades, generations, before we were successful, so we are perfectly prepared to wait them out."

I could not but admire his stoicism and sense of quiet commitment.

"Now," he emphasized, "you must carry our message back downriver to your superiors, and we will await their reply. We give them seventy-two hours, not a minute more!"

I turned my kayak smartly about for my return trip, and I noticed immediately that it moved with greater ease and speed. The Palisadian noticed it too.

"Now you can see for yourself," he called out to me, "how much easier it is when you are not paddling against the current of history!"

Help

The scent of scandal hung over the Capitol when it was discovered that the staff assistants of Senator Wimbol—secretaries, receptionists, statisticians, economists, parapsychologists, lawyers, and accountants—consisted in the main of illegal immigrants. Subsequent investigation revealed that they had been imported both by bus and by boat in the dead of night. They had been supplied with forged documents—working papers, residence permits, immunization certificates—and were employed at one third the salary usually paid native-born assistants of similar background and qualifications.

When agents of the Immigration and Naturalization Service appeared in the Senator's office to organize a mass deportation of the illegal aliens, there was much confusion and controversy. It seemed for a while that Wimbol's lengthy career hung in the balance. Accusations of racism and exploitation were hurled about. Labor unions protested. Law school faculties across the nation passed resolutions condemning the importation of cheap foreign labor which threatened to destroy the market for their new graduates. Agricultural cooperatives feared that the revolution of rising expectations would sweep the fruit fields, causing a mass exodus to Washington, where wages were higher and working conditions presumed to be better. Patriotic constituents of all political persuasions were horrified to discover that the laws which governed them were being drafted by foreigners. Editorialists theorized that the incomprehensibility of recent federal statutes was attributable to the fact that they had been written originally in Spanish and had lost something in translation.

In fact, the origins of the scandal were really quite innocent. It had been an especially busy time in the spring, and Wimbol and several colleagues had needed part-time help to cope with the sudden influx of correspondence and the heightened demand for congressional activity which, from time to time, seizes the nation. Reliable Agency, Inc., had been well recommended, having been in the business of supplying supplementary custodial help to the Capitol complex for more than a century. Indeed, the firm had begun as a placement service for newly freed slaves after the Civil War. Over the decades, its business had expanded, and the agency became one of the capital city's principal conduits for aspiring groups. Its slogan, "Rely on Reliable for Rapid Social Mobility," was prominently displayed inside the Greyhound bus station—that famous jumping-off point for many a great Washington career of the modern era.

The key to Reliable's success was its pioneering role in the system of day-splitting. Graduates of Guatemala's most prestigious college of law, who were usually hired out at the day rate of twenty-five dollars per day, could strain the average senator's office budget. Most often, the accumulated legislative mess took no more than two half days a week to clean up. Accordingly, senators would arrange among themselves the sharing of such lawyer-like help, and would also decide how to apportion the additional fees for lunch and carfare which had to be paid. One wretched Guatemalan, caught in the roundup in Senator Wimbol's office, explained that he would work two thirds of a day per week for Wimbol, half a week for the Architect of the Capitol, and would then pick up such odd jobs as were available. "But I would never work for Senator Wiggins again" (one of the two lady senators), he explained. "She is too fierce a señora, always following you around the office, making sure you have looked under all the desks for unanswered letters, getting on your back if the 'in' box is even the tiniest bit fuller than the 'out' box, always complaining about the dust on the desks. I swear by Our Lady of Guadaloupe, I never going to set foot in that place even one more time."

It was surely unseemly that the Capitol had become the site for a midnight raid by immigration agents. It had been hoped that the well-publicized dragnet would act as a deterrent to prospective employee and employer alike, but the practice was more deeply established than had been realized at the time. The roundups soon became a near-weekly occurrence, conducted under the glare of klieg lights and within range of television cameras. How could this subversive influx be contained? Some proposed the construction of an electrified fence to surround the Capitol grounds. Others proposed that the problem be solved through direct negotiations with the Latin-American governments involved. Still others proposed a straightforward arrangement which would link the employment of illegal Central Americans on Capitol Hill directly to Mexican oil and gas exports to the United States. But the majority favored the appointment of a Presidential Commission.

It was about this time that attention was diverted from the problem of Latin Americans by the appearance, in ever-increasing numbers, of so-called boat people from Southeast Asia. It was reported that a small flotilla of Chinese junks had entered the mouth of the Potomac River and was slowly making its way upriver to the Federal City. The Navy and the Coast Guard had been alerted, for the intentions of the newcomers were not at all obvious. A huge cast-iron chain was stretched across the river just beyond the boundary of the District of Columbia. The guns of the battleship U.S.S. *New Jersey*—hurriedly removed from mothballs to cope with the new crisis—were trained on the junks. The naval vessels signaled each other with semaphore and heliograph.

When the lead junk was no more than a thousand yards from the chain, the Admiral of the Capital District, standing in the prow of his flagship, spoke through his bullhorn. "Heave to and state your business. You are now well within the territorial waters of the United States of America and subject to the full and awesome authority of the Government of the United States—and each of its three branches, for that matter, especially the Judiciary, if you are determined to file suit."

"We appreciate the fulsomeness of this welcome," said the captain of the lead junk, "an appropriate ceremony for one's former brothers in the common battle against Bolshevism."

"There is some suspicion," replied the Admiral of the Capital District, "that you may be entering the country illegally, that you lack the proper documentation, and that you may be depriving other illegal entrants of their hard-won opportunity to secure useful employment on Capitol Hill."

"Oh, nothing so grandiose as all that," answered the headman of the boat people contingent. "We are prepared to start at the bottom—positions at the Federal Mediation and Conciliation Service perhaps."

"Ah," said the Admiral through his bullhorn, "in that case you are more than welcome." And, with that, he signaled a large barge owned by Reliable Agency, Inc., to come forward and to begin taking the names of the new arrivals.

When the barons of Capitol Hill heard of this episode, they besieged Reliable with requests for office help. For their part, they had had enough of the laid-back ways of the Latins. "Besides," as Senator Wimbol later remarked, "our Spanish-speaking friends seem to have priced themselves out of the market."

The Eleventh Man

The Soviet Secret Service activated the most effective spy network it had ever established in any capital when it finally succeeded in installing one of its agents as the head of the meatcutting department of Washington's largest supermarket. Carefully and painfully, the enemy's spy masters had infiltrated their agents first into frozen foods, then produce, and then dairy products. They had encountered their first difficulties in the delicatessen section, but those too had been overcome. However, the counterintelligence procedures of the meatcutting department had been difficult to crack. Moreover, the departments in their internal operations were kept separate; it was difficult for one agent to help another. But spies are a patient and silent lot, and Soviet persistence finally paid off when the management agreed that Perry Sharpe should be promoted.

None had suspected Sharpe's political sympathies. He had,

to all appearances, been a man of conventional politics. He had thought his property taxes too high and his residential garbage pickup too infrequent. Such grousing, however, masked a thoroughly revolutionary attitude. In his youth, when he was first recruited by the opposition, he had thought that his greatest contribution to the Socialist "motherland" would be to study high-energy physics and infiltrate the Pentagon's most secret weapons programs. But his control officer, who had been in charge of his espionage training at a secret school somewhere in the East, had given him another assignment. "We are top-heavy with physicists, *tovarich*," he had said. "What we need is meatcutters, a trade for which we have a particular affection in any case."

"Why do you need meatcutters?" asked Sharpe.

"It is not your worry, *tovarich*. Wait patiently, and you will know," said the spy master.

Sharpe always obeyed orders. He was also motivated to become an outstanding meatcutter, the best in his class in fact. He received the choicest assignments after he went to work at the supermarket. He knew that sooner or later he would be called upon to perform great and outstanding services for the Revolution.

In preparation for his great work, Sharpe kept up on the latest developments in espionage and continued to hone his skills. One day he was summoned secretly to a rendezvous in the dead of night at the end of a dark and obscure alley in downtown Washington. "We have heard of your promotion," said the mysterious man from the East, "and we are now in a position to spring the greatest espionage trap of modern times." Sharpe was excited by the prospect, and yet he eagerly sought an explanation.

"You can now know why you have been sent here and given your assignment," said the spy master. "For several years our leaders in the Kremlin have become increasingly dissatisfied with the quality of political intelligence they have been receiving from the United States. We have studied this problem and probed our inadequacies. We have concluded that the best source of information in all of America is the su-

permarket. It has therefore been decided that we will gradually assume control over the staff of every supermarket in
America. Soon every checker, every produce handler, every
stamper of cans, every distributor of free samples of new
cheese will be reporting directly to us."

Sharpe gasped, overcome by the enormity of the conception. Yes, it had been right there under his very nose for all
those years, and yet he had never seen it. Had he not personally conversed with the most important persons in Washington as they requested that extra fat be trimmed from a leg of
lamb? Did not important ambassadors, especially from the
strategic Middle East, handle the peaches and pinch the ba-
nanas, and engage the weighers of produce in conversation
about the state of the world? Could not a sharp-eared checker
overhear the most sensitive details of the intimate conversations the matrons of Washington conducted with each other
as they waited in line, waiting for the checker to point the
laser beam at the bizarre design known as the Universal Product Marking Code? And could not all those pieces of information be pieced together back in the Kremlin, so that the complex mosaic of Washington political life could be seen for the
unified, though intricate, pattern that it was?

"Brilliant," exclaimed Sharpe. "With such genius, it is obvious that victory will surely belong to the struggling masses of
the world."

"Knock it off," said the spy master. "Supermarket personnel,
especially those in the meat department, don't talk that way.
Be careful, or you'll blow your cover."

Having been properly rebuked, Sharpe awaited further instruction. "I can tell you," said the spy master, "that the
Washington Supermarket has now been infiltrated to the
point where it can become our most valuable listening post in
the Western Hemisphere. And you, Sharpe, are to be in
charge, the coordinator, the sifter, the chief. And, if you suc-
ceed, there'll be a medal in it for you, I promise you that."

"I wish only to be of service to the cause," said Sharpe
humbly.

The first payoff for the painstaking plot was not long in

coming. The Soviets were the first to deduce that Mexico would reverse its traditional policy and join OPEC when the chef at the Mexican Embassy appeared at the meat counter late Saturday afternoon in an agitated state. He said that the Ambassador had wanted to serve loin of pork that evening, but that the unexpected acceptance of an invitation required that loin of pork be abandoned in favor of rack of lamb. The unexpected alliance between India and China had also been foretold in a similar way, when three chefs from the Chinese Embassy were observed purchasing two large tins of curry powder. The Egyptian Embassy, which hitherto had purchased Manischewitz White Concord Wine for its Sunday-morning brunches, switched rather abruptly to Italian Swiss Colony Chardonay, foreshadowing the dramatic reversal of alliances in the Middle East which triggered the most recent war in that region. Correctly anticipating that Italy would remain neutral and that Switzerland would remain banker for both sides, the Soviets were able to make a major killing on the Tel Aviv stock exchange—by selling short in advance of the eruption of hostilities. Moreover, it was always apparent when the U. S. Navy was about to undertake long maneuvers, since the wife of the Chief of Naval Operations would purchase several cans of shaving cream for her husband in the supermarket, because the shaving cream was cheaper in the supermarket than it was at the drugstore next door.

The Supermarket Sircus, as it was secretly known in KGB headquarters in Moscow, continued to supply one intelligence scoop after the other. One particularly alert checker overheard the hushed confession of one female teen-ager to another that she had become pregnant as a result of a liaison with one of the elevator operators in the Washington Monument. The KGB was able to blackmail the operator—for the teen-ager was the child of a socially prominent cigar store owner who could have made big trouble for the hapless operator if the news got out—into allowing the installation of sensitive listening devices inside the top of the monument. With this sophisticated apparatus, the Russians were able to eavesdrop on the conversations of tens of thousands of Americans as they waited in line for White House tours at the height of the various tourist seasons. In fact, the Russians knew far in advance of the President himself what would, and what would not, play in Peoria. The Russians adjusted their propaganda accordingly, and they were soon unusually popular in Peoria, such that ordinary Peorians began to reassure each other that the Russians were really as American as apple pie.

Needless to say, the series of foreign policy reverses suffered by the United States as a result of this espionage was a cause of concern at the very highest level. It was suspected that a "mole"—an enemy agent under the deepest cover—had somehow burrowed into the upper reaches of the government. Counterintelligence agents were put on the case. They were unable to discover whether a mole had burrowed into the upper reaches of government, but they did discover that a large and complex warren existed beneath the White House, and that the warren was inhabited by three dozen rabbits. When the Office of Anticounter Intelligence submitted this report of its findings to the President, the Commander in Chief promptly fired the Director of OAI on the grounds that the man was a hopeless moron. The task was farmed out instead to the Bureau of Anticounter Intelligence, whose Director was, of course, the legendary X. (X, as is known, is a direct descendant of the same X who figured so prominently in the XYZ Affair of the late eighteenth century.)

X was not X for nothing. He decided to begin with the rabbits, since they constituted the only clue he had. He assumed that if there were rabbits under the White House, someone had to be feeding them, and that, if they were normal rabbits, they probably liked lettuce and carrots. He placed the rabbits under surveillance. He soon noticed that once or twice a week a known Soviet KGB agent, attached to the Soviet Embassy, would throw a bunch of carrots on the ground after he finished picnicking in the small park across the street from the White House. One of the rabbits would then emerge, retrieve the carrots, scurry back under the White House fence, and return to the warren. What did this mean? The carrots, which were intercepted by government agents, contained no messages of any sort. In any case, the process would have to work in reverse, for one would expect that it would be the rabbits who were carrying messages to the Russians, not vice versa.

X was stumped. However, a tail on the Russian agent revealed the fact that he bought a bunch of carrots every Tuesday at the supermarket. "There must be some link here," X reasoned. He decided to take an enormous gamble. He ordered the Russian apprehended in the supermarket's parking lot. The carrots were subjected to the closest scrutiny, and were found to contain well-hidden microdots, cleverly concealed in the green stuff at the top of the bunch. "So that is why he threw away those perfectly good carrots," said X. He then decided that someone in the supermarket was placing the microdots in the carrots, and using the carrots to get the information to the Russians. Additional surveillance of the employees of the supermarket pinpointed the chief of the produce department as the culprit. He, too, was apprehended, and he broke under interrogation, saying in his defense that he had begun life as a migrant farm worker who picked carrots and had become radicalized in the process. Within days, ten members of the ring were under detention. Each spoke mysteriously of the existence of a so-called eleventh man, but no one knew his identity.

As for Perry Sharpe, he had grown uneasy as he watched his subordinates picked off one by one by his nemesis, X. He feared that his own cover would sooner or later be blown. The Russians concurred. He was spirited out of the United States and given a fine residence for his retirement in Moscow.

But Sharpe soon became bored. He realized that he was no longer of use as a spy, but could he not be of some use in the effort to build socialism in the U.S.S.R. nonetheless? He asked for employment in Moscow as a meatcutter, but his hosts continued to stall. He continued to press them.

At long last, they revealed the bitter truth. "We have no

further use for you, *tovarich* Sharpe, and you might as well adjust to it," explained one of his hosts. "Once again, our state statistical bureau has informed us of one of the annual anomalies of our system. It is this simple: We have a surplus of meatcutters, but a shortage of meat."

Propositions

Political observers have noted the tendency toward a resolution of important public questions nowadays by direct vote in referenda. This practice is assumed to have begun in California, the birthplace of the famous Proposition Thirteen. But the practice is well established in democratic societies. So far as one can tell, the custom was begun in the golden age of Greek civilization when the first Proposition, Proposition Alpha, was submitted to the voters. It had to do with how landholdings should be surveyed for the purpose of computing the local property tax. The Proposition on the ballot read as follows:

"In any right triangle, shall the square of the hypotenuse be equal to the sum of the squares of the other two sides?"

Fortunately, almost 90 percent of the Athenians voted "yes," thereby sparing students of geometry any serious controversy until well into the nineteenth century. But it had not

always been thus. The City Fathers had tried to ram through
an ordinance requiring that the square of the hypotenuse be
larger than the sum of the squares of the other two sides. A
tax revolt was launched.

It was not until the tax revolt spread to the United States
that people began to understand that political science really
was a science after all, or at least related to great developments in science. Warren Bradgen, a professor of the history
of political science at Washington's best university, has allowed us to understand how we have been thrown off the
track all these years. "Because," he writes, "the Declaration of
Independence had the good sense to speak of *self-evident*
truths, no referendum needed to be held. But the more we
probe into the surviving data and documents, the more we
discover a well-established sequence: scientific proposition
first, popular ratification second, political action a poor third."
The results of this research have now appeared in a nicely
bound monograph, and it provides no shortage of insights.

Everyone knows that the American Revolution was
influenced by the Glorious Revolution in Britain, which occurred in 1688, about the time Sir Isaac Newton was seeking
converts to his new way of looking at things. When the First
Continental Congress met in 1775, this was still an open question. Benjamin Franklin submitted the following question to
the populace:

"Shall a body at rest be allowed to remain at rest unless
acted upon by an outside force?"

Seventy-three percent voted "no," thereby authorizing the
delegates to disturb both the mind and the body of George
III by rebelling.

Yet, it took almost a century before another of Newton's
important axioms was submitted to the voters. The controversy arose about 1850, when California wished to become a
member of the Union. At that time, California was separated
from the rest of the United States by about a thousand miles
—the distance has since grown—and it was necessary to determine once and for all whether the nation would answer
"yes" to the following question:

"Shall particles of matter be allowed to attract each other with a force that varies directly as the product of their masses and inversely as the square of the distance between them?"

The stakes were large. Failure to ratify would throw all of astronomical research into great confusion, but if the voters did not turn down the Law of Gravity, "Manifest Destiny" would suffer a mortal blow. Ratification would mean nothing less than an admission that distant places could not be strongly attracted to the United States. Happily, sane heads prevailed. The Proposition was narrowly defeated, and California joined the Union. And by directly bucking popular scientific trends of the day, the Americans of 1850 made possible not only the admission of California, but also the subsequent admission of Alaska and Hawaii, the annexation of the Philippines and Puerto Rico and, later, the Vietnam War.

Inevitably, supporters of the Proposition have come to look upon the admission of California to the Union as a victory of "know-nothingism." Professor Bradgen disputes this claim, noting that the American voter is perfectly happy to support the findings of science, no matter how bizarre they appear on their face, when an important question of the national interest is involved. This is especially true during wartime. Thus, when a group of funny-talking physicists arrived in America and began to talk about an ultimate weapon, the following Propositon was considered:

"Shall the energy in any atom be expressed as the amount of its mass multiplied by the square of the speed of light?"

Given the secrecy surrounding the issue, no one could be told why he was being asked to vote upon so obscure an item. But the voters took it on faith. Eighty-one percent of them voted "yes" and the Manhattan Project was funded.

The modern American economy rests on the wisdom of the Governors of the Federal Reserve System. The Federal Reserve, as anyone who has crammed for the New York State Regents Examination has learned, was proposed by President Woodrow Wilson. But before this awesome step could be taken, the voters were asked to determine once and for all the answers to two Propositions that had been raised in 1803 by the great French mathematician Adrien-Marie Legendre. The ballot read as follows:

"If k and a be two relatively prime integers with $k>2$, and the arithmetic progression, a sequence of integers beginning with a, is considered, then:

(1) Are there infinitely many primes in this progression, i.e., are there infinitely many $p \equiv a \pmod k$?

(2) If so, and $\pi (a, k, x)$ be the number of such primes $\leqq x$, then if $(a_1k) = (a_2k) = 1$, is it true that a limiting expression for a ratio of functions π equals 1? That is, are the numbers of primes in the different residue classes modulo k equidistributed?"

The voters answered with a thumping "yes" to both questions, thereby making it possible for the Federal Reserve to calculate the prime rate.

Since then, there has been only one other important matter of this sort to enter into the political process. This had to do with the establishment of Big Government. Before Big Government could come into being, the Senate had to ratify a treaty whereby the United States agreed to be bound by the Third Law of Thermodynamics. Briefly stated, this Law says that, in any system, heat tends to flow from areas of greater concentration to areas of lesser concentration, with the result that everything in the system soon winds down to a temperature of absolute zero (about −500 degrees or so). If this Law were true, then the establishment of Big Government would be not only necessary but inevitable. Fortunately, the Senate grasped the truth of this Proposition, and things have been cooling down rather nicely ever since.

For all of this, as Professor Bradgen points out, we are indebted to an obscure British philosopher of medieval times, John of Occam. Occam is best known for Occam's Razor, a cardinal rule of political life, which states: "Do not multiply explanations beyond necessity." Occam has since become a consultant to the Office of Management and Budget.

The Quiet Revolution

I remember well how our current condition of peace, prosperity, and happiness originated in the political malaise of 1980. In those days, we didn't understand the sources of our discontent. Now, of course, we know better. This very week, we're celebrating another anniversary of our *Fundamental Statute,* which, not a moment too soon, vested all legislative, executive, and judicial power in the Executive Secretary of the Board of Directors of the Aspen Institute for Humanistic Studies.

It had been a startling development, quite unexpected. Even hardheaded war-gamers had overlooked the growing influence of The Institute, especially after its famous seminar, "Creative Necrology and Pre-emptive Bioethics," had opened sectarian fissures. The future of structural humanism seemed to hang in the balance. All the more remarkable, then, was The Institute's continued rise to its position of pre-eminent World Power.

It was managed with consummate skill. The Executive Secretary was a retiring man who had begun with skimpy resources: two bamboo ski poles, some frayed bindings, a pair of shabby boots, a rickety chair lift, a small A-frame in Colorado—small, yet well stocked with the Great Books of the Western (and the Eastern and Southern and Northern and Under) World. But he had vision and unshakable self-confidence.

"I never had any doubts," the Executive Secretary said when he announced that he would rule with the title of Humanist-General. And he gestured to the enormous oil portrait on the wall of his study. It was Mortimer Adler. "That's my first seminarist painted on the wall, looking as if he were alive. Will't please you to sit and look at him?" he would say to all first-time visitors. But it was the Humanist-General whose earnest glance showed depth and passion.

Later on, the Humanist-General could talk calmly of the sensational scandal that had almost sidetracked him. That was the huge commotion caused by the leaking of The Institute's famous ten-year plan, *The Protocols of the Elders of Aspen*. Written in Esperanto and containing a preface signed in a near-illegible scrawl (thought to be that of Wendell Willkie), the *Protocols* created a near-panic.

Well they might have. The document was nothing less than a detailed blueprint for the seizure of world power, for the establishment of a new super-government on the ruins of the world system. "Naturally, we had to denounce it as a forgery and launch a massive public relations counterattack. It was a trying period, the greatest challenge to our doctrine of creative non-momentous philology. I recall that I was chairing our international seminar on the life of Paramahansa Yogananda and its implications for landscape architecture when the story broke. Premature disclosure could have wiped out thirty years of hard work. But I didn't panic.

"I had been against drawing up the *Protocols* from the beginning," continued the Humanist-General with an ever so slight Colorado drawl. "We didn't need a turgid text. Maybe our plans seemed a little advanced for their day, but it surely has worked out all right. Besides, everyone knew—or should have known—what we were doing. We had open meetings; we had our own airstrip to receive visitors; we spoke on National Public Radio; we made records for the blind and movies for the deaf. Everyone who was anyone came to our place in the mountains. Then we bought some seaside villas and they came there. Then they came to our town houses, our campgrounds, our trailer parks, and our houseboats. It was only a matter of time until all segments of American society would be educated, organized, and directed by The Institute."

He said this during his first televised interview with Barbara Walters, and he made known his resolve to use his extraordinary powers with dignity, grace, and restraint. "You know," he said to Miss Walters, "sometimes up in the mountains, after a hard day of grappling with the complex issues of our variegated culture, it's nice to sit around the campfire, relax, and maybe even sing a song or two." And with that, he reached for his guitar, and sang his now legendary theme song, with its haunting refrain:

(To the tune of "Rocky Mountain High")

In the Colorado Rockies bye and bye
On pungent globalism we'll get high
We'll teach you how things came to be
So you'll never have to wonder why
Aspen's mountain high

In the Colorado Rockies it's no lie
We've seen it raining insights from the sky
Where things are just as plain as day
So the CIA need never spy
Aspen's mountain high

The past years have shown him as good as his word. Even bitter-enders who resisted the ascendancy of The Institute are now among the first to acknowledge that he was right from the start, and not a bit fuzzy on the issues.

For who among the leading journalists and commentators had not been present at one or another Aspen seminar, high in the mountains? Was there a major corporate executive who had not been ferried in his Lear jet to delve into the necessary nexus between commerce and theologies? Who had not heard that Pascal's Wager had become the Planetary Bargain? Whose aesthetic sense had not been refined after hearing The Institute's own musicians perform eight-, ten-, twelve-, and fourteen-tone music?

And then there were the diplomats and financiers, politicians and professors, who had willingly confided the most intimate details of their lives to the Aspen Institute Oral History Project. None had suspected that this would become the basis for the notorious Aspen Dossiers.

Then The Institute began to coin its own money by special arrangement with the Franklin Mint of Philadelphia. The Aspenrand, as the coin came to be known, was backed by the staggering silver lode of The Institute's Colorado mines. Inevitably the Aspenrand became a rock of stability in an era of wild monetary fluctuation. The Gnomes of Zurich (actually the collateral branch of the famous family led by Herman and Isidore Gnome) were also drawn into The Institute's orbit. Together, they became the most powerful currency manipulators of the twentieth century.

In truth, the Executive Secretary had not been a creative economist. Instead, his forte was foreign policy, which allowed his imaginative genius free rein. He established affiliates in all the great capitals of Europe and Asia; he opened wholly owned subsidiaries throughout Africa and Latin America; he maintained tax shelters in New Hebrides and Barbados; he subscribed to *Le Monde*. With this extensive network of listening posts, he gathered startlingly accurate intelligence. His predictions of earthquakes and oil prices were uncanny. Fortunes were made and lost on the basis of information he provided. Governments urged him to take

over management of their dwindling foreign-exchange hold-
ings. In a brilliant *coup de main,* he obtained observer status
for The Institute at the United Nations General Assembly—
which then adopted by a vote of 116–9 (12 abstentions, 11
missing in action) a resolution declaring The Institute "the
sole legitimate representative of struggling optimists, ra-
tionalists, monetarists, and other oppressed peoples."

Meantime, it became necessary to create Aspen Security
Forces to protect The Institute's worldwide chain of facilities.
ASFO, as the armed component was known, soon numbered
more than 800,000, including naval and air elements. The au-
thoritative Institute of Strategic Studies in London reported
that ASFO had become the fourth-largest standing military
force in the world.

"You see," said the Humanist-General, "I knew what I was
doing."

Anyone who has read up on the Portrait Gallery Crisis can
hardly deny it! The neutralization of The Institute's *real* rivals
for global hegemony had required a series of dazzling maneuvers. "The key to it was my strategy of unite and conquer. I
secured the merger of the Brookings Institution with the
American Enterprise Institute, thereby allowing two potential
rivals to bore each other to death. Then—and this was a mas-
terstroke—I arranged for the Smithsonian Institution to absorb the surviving remnants, thereby creating a new organization, Smithbrook American. I, for one, had never
underestimated the Smithsonian; I knew it was much more
than the bag of old dinosaur bones it pretended to be. It was
on the move. But it never got deeply enough into foreign policy and, like the dinosaurs, its brain got too small for its
body."

A characteristic understatement about the epic struggle between The Institute and Smithbrook American for control of
the Northern Hemisphere! The Thirty Years' War was a tod-
dler's scuffle by comparison. What began as a simple request
by The Institute to purchase the subscription list of *Smithsonian* magazine erupted into bloody battle. But the outcome

was never in doubt. The Humanist-General made mincemeat of the Curator-General.

"Finally, we were where we wanted to be," the victor would later say, "*mano a mano* with the Trilateral Commission, just the two of us, eyeball to eyeball, in the great game for all the marbles—and they blinked. Then they shuddered; then they trembled; then they began to shake uncontrollably. In the end, they collapsed completely."

How had it happened? The Colorado Coup, as it came to be known, was really an anticlimactic letdown after all those years of combat. The Trilateral Commission, already a quadrilateral one in everything but name, had decided to skip stage five and move directly toward its first Hexagonal Conference. But it made the mistake of renting The Institute's lodge for the occasion. "Singularly naïve of them to think we would honor a flag of truce so that they might have their triennial septagonal seminar," chuckled the Humanist-General. "ASFO just rounded them up, and that was that. Frankly, I never did have much respect for the Trilaterals; no one ever named a station wagon after *them*."

No matter. The Humanist-General triumphed and he has since created a sense of order, serenity, and well-being unknown since the Era of Good Feeling. The vision of the Elders of Aspen has become a living reality. Throughout the world, people are coming to comprehend the connectedness of things. They are united in genuine awe of human intellectual and material achievement. They have come together. And they will make the critical choices.

Book II

GIVE EAR, ALL INHABITANTS
OF THE LAND

The Art of the Possible

Instant political analysis was finally vindicated and became properly accepted as an authentic art form with the opening of the Georgetown Gallery of Political Commentary. For years, connoisseurs, aficionados, collectors, and dealers had clamored for the status that only a real gallery could provide. Shrewd investors had seen the potential early on, as the price of other artifacts of our culture had soared beyond all reasonable expectations. The speculators moved in, and fortunes were made as these works changed hands. Thus, an original Lippmann, which only five years ago had nothing but curiosity value, was recently sold for several thousand dollars. In the finest of homes, it is now more than acceptable—it is in fact necessary—to display the better examples of the genre, suitably framed and mounted, sometimes placed between sheets of plastic and installed on small pedestals.

It is, of course, a field where the novice and the amateur

are easily taken by sharp operators. The shrewd collector will want to know exactly what he is getting, and the Georgetown Gallery was founded with such individuals clearly in mind. Indeed, the Catalogue of Artistic Commentary is an absolute must for anyone who contemplates investments in this new growth market.

As the catalogue points out, there are various schools and trends, many masters, and even more apprentices. The commentators work in many media, including cold type on unlined white paper, pen and ink on yellow legal-sized paper, paint and eyedropper on canvas, stylus on clay, and chisel in marble. This is not all easily understood, and it is necessary to begin at the beginning.

There are first of all, the *old masters*. The old masters take the long view and their best works were, and still are, composed on farms that they own in the countryside, far away from the hustle and bustle of everyday life. Their works are never done in watercolor, but only the oiliest of oils, so that they have from the outset a permanence which distinguishes them from the larger field. Old masters comment for old newspapers; they never comment on the back pages of weekly news magazines. This is best understood by citing an excerpt from a recent work by one of the old masters (one generally considered to be the Rembrandt of the school if the truth be told):

"There in the Nation's Capital, as seen from here in the nearby countryside, there is a mood of cautious optimism tempered by an air of prudent pessimism. The situation has changed from what it once was. Before the conventions, delegates were the name of the game; now the name of the game is electoral votes. If the pattern holds—and there is every reason to believe that the more populous states will continue to have more electoral votes than the smaller ones—the election will almost certainly determine the outcome. Historians here are trying to remember a time when the candidate with a majority of the electoral votes failed to win the election, and maybe they will remember such a time. But it could happen.

Supposing the election ended in a tie and was thrown into the House of Representatives, where each state has one vote. Given the fact that there are fifty states, we could easily have a twenty-five and twenty-five deadlock. Obviously, this argues for the admission of a fifty-first state, but which territory should it be? This is a bedeviling issue, and the candidates' silence on it may account for their current predicaments. However, the problem is not unique; we lived through it all those years when the Union had only forty-eight states, also an even number."

The catalogue points out that this work of art by an old master was sold to a noted collector, the publisher of an old newspaper, for $2,500.

Of course, there is no disputing taste. Not everyone treasures the old masters. There has been a measurable growth in the market for works by a newer school, the *fauves*, that is, the beasts. The catalogue also offers an extract from a recent piece of *fauve* commentary that was sold for $1,100:

"Staggered by repeated instances of idiocy, the candidate's campaign sustained another enormous blow as the result of a moronic miscue that has seasoned observers shaking their heads. The candidate's monumentally stupid gaffe occurred in plain sight, as harried aides came close to pulling out what remained of their hair. 'The jackass has stuck his foot down his throat once again,' one of the aides confided to me in a dimly-lit bar, 'and it's going to take one helluva effort to cover his tracks on this one.' But, of course, this is nothing new. Campaign veterans have gasped in disbelief as the candidate's campaign stumbles from one amateurish bungle to another. I raised this directly with the candidate himself, and I asked him point-blank: 'Do you really think people are going to vote for you given your propensity to make a complete ass of yourself every time you speak in public?' Hiding behind the cowardly code of the press corps, he requested to answer off the record, but believe you me, I am going to nail the dope when he's not on his guard!"

The *fauves* should not be taken as totally representative of the modernist school. For they compete with the *surrealists* for the interest of well-heeled buyers. A work by one of the better-known surrealists was recently auctioned off for several thousand dollars and it deserves a citation in this context:

"Politics has become more of a science than ever before in our history. Survey research and market research have had a near-revolutionary impact. But the science of politics is bound to make another quantum leap when the research of Professor Grant Wollston of Duke University is published this spring. Wollston has established an indisputable correlation between voting behavior on the one hand and the voter's biorhythmic patterns on the other. He advises all serious candidates to dispense with the questionnaire and instead sample the prospective voter's respiratory, circulatory, and metabolic rates. The lower these are, the less likely is the individual to vote, since he will lack the requisite physical energy to pull the lever or stuff in the ballot."

Less well-developed than surrealism is the school of *pointillism*. Pointillist commentary is distinguished by frequent use of the word "point," as in the following example:

"Politicians who make this point overlook several other points. The first of these points is point one, which is to say, the basic point, from which all other points follow: Politics is not pointless, but depends ultimately on one's point of view. This is a point worth pointing out."

Pointillism has given rise to yet another school, sometimes called the "connect the dots" school, which is another form really of the larger trend in political commentary toward *abstract expressionism*. The basic tenet of the abstract expressionist school is that the seemingly random points can be connected so as to reveal a pattern. Thus, a recent representative work of abstract expressionism began as follows:

"The news of the past week has been dominated by three developments, seemingly unrelated: the sudden abdication of Prince Rainier of Monaco, which followed upon riots in the principality triggered by a group of disgruntled losers at the gaming tables; a forest fire which has been raging out of control for the last seven weeks in the timberlands of the upper Amazon; and the discovery of leaks in the roof of the New Orleans Superdome. What ties these seemingly disparate events together in a single pattern, however, is the pattern of unpredictability, the seeming randomness of single events which reveal more to us about the tenor of our times than any of us ever expected. The only thing that is permanent is change itself, the only certainty is uncertainty, and even uncertainty itself will become obvious after it happens."

These samples do nothing but skim the surface. For the Georgetown Gallery has for sale the works of the *cubists,* who go beyond the two-dimensional surface of things and comment in real depth; the *impressionists,* who distrust the data of the Census Bureau whenever it conflicts with their own instincts; the *pop artists,* who understand the political significance of Campbell Soup and Brillo, and who are prone to use such terms as "wow" and "zoweee"; and the pure *modernists,* who turn in nothing but blank paper to their editors, because they believe that every citizen should think for himself. But none of this is cut and dried. The true geniuses in the field can move from one school to another. They tend to be optimistic about the future. But almost every one of them has had his *blue period.*

Interim Report

MEMORANDUM FOR THE PRESIDENT

From: Executive Director, Blue Ribbon Commission on National Philosophy Policy

Subject: Toward a National Philosophy Policy

I have the honor to submit the first interim report of
the Blue Ribbon Commission on National Philosophy Policy,
authorized by Public Law 94-971, with members appointed by
your predecessor. You will recall that the authorizing statute
charges the Commission with answering certain specific questions. This Interim Report summarizes tentative conclusions
only. The staff of the Commission has not yet completed its
sifting of the documents and testimony presented to it. So
much material! It could fill a library!

1) *What is the role of the federal government in establishing a National Philosophy Policy?*

We believe that the American people deserve a clear, comprehensive, coordinated—need we add rational?—National
Philosophy Policy, as clear, comprehensive, coordinated—
need we add rational?—as the American people themselves.
You have defined the National Purpose; accordingly, there
should also be a National Philosophy Policy.

2) *Who are the American people's favorite philosophers?*

The favorite philosophers of the American people are as diverse, differential, determined (maybe), and demographic as
the American people themselves. Our survey research shows a
marked preference among German-Americans for Kant and
Hegel. Jews—and Unitarians—show a similar preference for
Martin Buber. A preference for Machiavelli and Croce corre-
lates highly with the insistence, among certain groups, that
there is no Mafia. There is a 71 per cent probability that the
mere mention of Ortega y Gasset to a Spanish-surnamed
American will cause him to yell, "*¡Viva la Causa!*" On the
other hand, middle Americans exhibit great regard for Locke
and Mill. However, the favorite philosopher of the American
people—and by the same consistently wide margin—remains
Leo Durocher.

3) *Should philosophers be appointed to high positions in
the government?*

Definitely. Indeed, a certain number of the highest positions
should be reserved exclusively for philosophers, with propor-
tional representation for all schools. (The staff of the Commission is at work developing a formula to achieve this.) Em-
piricism is the dominant school, especially in the field of
epistemology. The Commission's headquarters frequently
have been picketed by demonstrators chanting, "What you see
is what you get!" This issue is dealt with in a separate appen-
dix.

However, it is the Commission's unanimous view that the
position of Principal Foreign Policy Adviser to the President

should never be filled by a philosopher. In keeping with now well-established precedent, it should be filled only by a foreign-born linguistic anthropologist.

4) *Can we learn from History or are we condemned to repeat it?*

The relevant documents concerning the Commission's deliberations on this sensitive question were lost in a tragic fire. Arson is suspected. Meanwhile, the staff cannot remember the Commission's conclusions.

5) *Does Art follow Life, or does Life follow Art?*

The Commission, after much digging, has established a clear relationship between the two. Much depends on the source of the artist's grant. Recently, those who have been getting their money from the Ford Foundation have shown a tendency toward socialist realism. Those who worked on a straight commission basis for Nelson Rockefeller are something else again. And people who take from Joseph Coors are yet a third category. A sensible artist will not bite the hand that feeds him.

The Commission's survey research shows considerable support for the right to Life, much less support for the right to Art. The executive branch needs to be reorganized to reflect this preference. In that there already exists a National Endowment for the Arts, the Commission recommends the creation of a National Endowment for Life—or maybe the evolution of a National Endowment for Life.

6) *Does man's ability to do sums support Aristotle's contention that man is rational because he can do sums?*

The Commission is as yet unable to render an opinion. Mr. Hunt has not yet replied to the Commission's questionnaire.

7) *As for man's relationship with other animals, is the difference one of kind or of degree?*

The evidence is not especially encouraging. The Commission has made a careful study of experiments which seek to establish communication with porpoises. Clearly, open politics requires that everyone—and everything—become involved in the process. The animals have much to teach us about how to live together in energy-efficient communities, about how to relate to the biosphere, about the delicate ecological balance. The Commission considers it prudent to keep an open mind about where we came from and where we are headed.

8) *Is it time to move beyond Freedom and Dignity?*

The Commission has concluded that this is far from inevitable. Freedom and Dignity will be preserved if sufficient incentives are written into the tax code.

9) *Is there a need for further research?*

The Commission believes there is need for much more research. Particularly bedeviling is the issue of why there is Anything instead of Nothing—or whether Everything is in fact Anything or whether it is really Nothing as some suppose. If you assume—as the Commission did—that there is Something, then it should be a small matter to tote up Everything. On the other hand, if there is Something, how can there be Nothing at the same time?

Accordingly, we must continue the search for Nothing, so as to find out whether Nothing exists. For this purpose, we recommend an appropriation of $611 million. We further recommend that the funds previously appropriated for the study of life after death be impounded, it now generally being known that such life exists. No one, however, has offered a satisfactory response to Alexander King's inquiry: Is there a life after birth? And, if there is, is it life as we know it, or is it the kind of life one finds on Mars, *viz.*, life as we do not know it?

10) *Is the shortage of Natural Philosophy real or contrived?*

The shortage is real and not contrived. The Commission believes that adequate supplies of Natural Philosophy can be made available for the winter if the price of Natural Philosophy is decontrolled at the godhead.

Book Review

The Congressman Who Loved Heidegger and Other Stories
by Grendel Smith
Reviewed by Rowena Harband

      My husband, the late Franklin Harband—known as the Judge—served in the Congress for twenty-seven years, before succumbing to the case of amoebic dysentery he contracted during his fact-finding tour of the Himalayan kingdoms this past autumn. But I have found a new life for myself as reviewer of political fiction for the Washington *Press,* and I want to thank all of my many friends who have encouraged me to take on this new assignment. This is the first book review I have ever written! I'm keeping my fingers crossed, even as I type—no easy feat—and with a gulp or two, here goes!

      Everybody knows that Grendel Smith is one of the most re-

spected journalists in this town. My late husband thought
highly of him, as did most of our friends. That's why I hope
he won't take it personally if I say that I didn't much care for
his book. Maybe I just don't understand it, but the people he
writes about sure aren't like anybody I've ever known.

Take the hero of the title story, for example. It's about a
congressman who tries to cope with his mid-life crisis by reading the works of all the famous European philosophers of the
twentieth century. It turns out that his favorite among them is
a German man named Martin Heidegger, who, according to
an encyclopedia I consulted, was something called a phenom-
enologist. According to Mr. Smith's story, the protagonist,
Congressman Bartley Trill, is immediately converted to phenomenology after reading Mr. Heidegger's most famous work,
Being and Time. He announces on the floor of the House of
Representatives that he has become a born-again phenomenol-
ogist, and announces that all of his colleagues are welcome at
a monthly phenomenology breakfast that he will host. He also
announces that since the force of the original doctrine is lost
in translation, he will speak nothing but German during future legislative debates. "I am no longer interested in bills as
such," he says, "but rather in the bill-in-itself, its bill-ness, so
to speak. We have to recover the essence of bill-ness if we are
ever to move toward a truly liberating, consciousness-ridden
creative jurisprudence." He talks like this for six months, until
one of his colleagues tells him that Heidegger, though an eminent philosopher, was actually a supporter of Adolf Hitler.
This upsets the congressman very much, and when he enrolls
in another semester of night school, he changes his major to
art history. What is the author trying to tell us in this story?
To tell the truth, it just went right by me.

Another interesting story in this collection is called "For
Whom the Bike Rolls." It's a story about another socially concerned congressman who gives up his gas-guzzling automobile
for a small moped, and the interesting people he meets when
he rides to and from the office. I read this story three times
before I realized that it was an allegory about the energy cri-

sis, how we never really get to know other people until we stop wasting gasoline. But the ending is hard to understand because, in the end, the moped is eaten by a large papier-mâché dragon during a Chinese New Year's parade. What is the author trying to tell us in this story? The key to it is in the last sentence when the author says, quite plainly, "Do not ask for whom the bike rolls." Mr. Smith is obviously striving for ambiguity.

Another interesting story is about a man with an unusual occupation. He is the night watchman at a hydrogen bomb warehouse. Every night, he has to count all the hydrogen bombs there to make sure none is missing. One night, he happens to be reading a magazine which has printed an article on how to make a hydrogen bomb. Suddenly, his curiosity is aroused. He realizes that he has been the night watchman for seventeen years and hasn't a clue as to how a hydrogen bomb is made. After he is finished taking the inventory, he decides to open up one of the bombs to see whether it really looks like the diagram printed in the magazine. But shortly after he removes the protective casing, his gold wedding ring comes into contact with a loose wire inside the mechanism and the bomb goes off. Miraculously, the night watchman survives, even though several square miles of surrounding countryside are incinerated. Giving thanks to God for his miraculous escape, he vows never to tamper with the secrets of the universe. This story is very realistic and convincing, as far as I am concerned. And I couldn't help but think that it is something of a miracle that we have never had this kind of a horrible accident in real life.

On the other hand, I don't know why Mr. Smith has one of his stories printed in the language of the Arapaho. He explains in an introductory footnote that American Indians need to have the "system" explained to them in their own tongue, so that they can relate to it. But how about people like your reviewer, who can't read Arapaho? I just suggest that you skip this one piece, because you'll find that no matter how hard you struggle, you won't be able to make heads or tails of it.

I have to admit that one of the things Mr. Smith does very cleverly indeed is to weave a religious message into his stories. I think he deals very nicely with the subtle interplay of religion and politics in our culture. Two of his stories deal with this head on. In the first, all of America's Roman Catholic cardinals meet secretly in the archdiocese of Washington. They are planning the national tour of the first American Pope. They want his trip to be a big success in the Midwest especially, and so they want a photograph of him savoring the American National Dish. But they cannot agree on what the American National Dish is. Those who argue that it is the Big Mac agree that it would be undignified to photograph the Supreme Pontiff biting into a large hamburger. They argue throughout the evening and well into the morning. The prelates become exhausted, and their meeting dissolves in bitter recrimination. I think the author is trying to tell us that in a diverse country like ours, it is a mistake to try and make everyone eat the same thing.

In the second story with a religious motif, the local elders of the Mormon Church gather at their tabernacle in nearby Maryland. They have been alerted that a major revelation is in the offing, and they have come to hear it. But when the message comes, they can't understand it. So they ask that it be repeated while they make a recording of it on a cassette. They take the cassette to nine eminent linguists, none of whom can recognize the language in which the revelation is spoken. On the tenth attempt, they are told that the voice is speaking in Yiddish. They refuse to accept this. Finally, they ask Washington's most distinguished rabbi to translate the message for them, and he does. The story ends, but we never find out what the revelation was! This, I think, is very significant. Maybe Mr. Smith wants to make the point that it is very difficult to know what God is saying to us. That may not be the right interpretation, but it certainly has been my own personal experience.

I wish Mr. Smith had written more about religion and less about sex, but I suppose he had to write about it, things being

what they are these days. I am more than a little embarrassed
to bring this up at all, but my editors here at the *Press* say
that I have to be honest in discussing this book and, to tell the
truth, I think I am basically an honest person. Frankly, I think
it is very hard to write about sex in a book without being
filthy and disgusting, and maybe even perverted, and I am
sorry to have to report that Mr. Smith has put some smut in
this collection. Besides, I think he's making it all up. Talk
about having an author's imagination run wild! He has a story
in the book called "The Congressman Who Made Love on
Mondays." It's about a congressman who comes home on
Monday nights, watches the Monday football game, and then
makes love to his wife. He does this only during the football
season; during the baseball and basketball seasons, he is continent. At first I thought that the author was trying to make a
point about sex and violence. But it's just an excuse to publish
pornography. On one Monday night, for example, he describes the goings-on in great detail, and actually quotes the
wife of the congressman as saying "ooh, ooh, ah, ah!" This is
wholly lacking in realism. I myself was married for more than
thirty years to my sainted Franklin and, in all the times we
came together in conjugal union, I never once said "ooh, ooh,
ah, ah," and I bet no one else ever did either. The most I can
remember saying is "ah, ooh," and that was only because the
window was open and a cold draft was coming in.

   All in all, there are sixteen stories in this collection, and I
don't have enough space to discuss all of them. Even though I
didn't care much for the book as a whole, I think the individual stories are worth reading. For people who have never
been to Washington, I think they'll learn that life here isn't
much different from life in most other places, even though it
is unique in some respects. Also I hope Mr. Smith doesn't get
too angry at me over what I've written here, because he is a
very dear man and I would like to keep him as a friend.

Culture

The Committee for the Preservation of Cultural Pluralism won a great victory when it secured, rent free, the use of the John F. Kennedy Center for the Performing Arts for its special two-week festival. The Committee was founded only a year ago, with the stated purpose of purging racism from the performing arts in the District of Columbia. This would be no easy task, given the oppressed condition of Caucasian culture in the District. But parents and teachers had become concerned that young Caucasians, seeing that performers of their background were underrepresented on the Kennedy Center's stages, would conclude that the performing arts—like basketball—were just not for them. "We must," said Mrs. Chadwick Grently, "attack the incipient problem of Wasp low self-esteem at its root."

The National Foundation for the Arts was reluctant to become involved—but what bureaucracy would not be? Then,

there was controversy aplenty. But the success of the endeavor has now led to unrestrained backslapping all around.
"It was a novel idea," said Leonard Waltztin, director of minority programs at the Foundation, and once reluctant to
comment on-the-record. "Mrs. Grently said that she wanted to
produce a series of all-white productions of famous black clas-
sics. After all, she had argued, there was an all-black version
of *Carmen—Carmen Jones*—and an all-black version of *The
Wizard of Oz—The Wiz*—and Alvin Ailey was hard at work
on an all-black production of *Fiddler on the Roof*. Why not
give someone else a chance?"

"The fact is," Mrs. Grently had argued, "the black cultural
experience must be made relevant to white children. That is
why we picked, as our first effort, the famous Fats Waller musical, *Ain't Misbehavin'*. The title was the first problem—
should it be *Aren't Misbehaving, Isn't Misbehaving*, or *Am I
Not Misbehaving?* How ever does one achieve communication
across historically inherited chasms of language and experience?"

Two months later, *Aren't Misbehaving* opened to a rare
critical acclaim. With this initial success the Foundation
moved boldly to underwrite the first all-white production of
Porgy and Bess, with the new title of *Padraic and Elizabeth*.
Robert Redford came out of the environmental movement to
sing the role of Padraic, and Cheryl Teigs, after months of
special voice instruction, was able to handle the difficult score
that Gershwin had written for Elizabeth. (Don Rickles appeared as Sporting Life.) "Particularly moving," wrote Saul
Tunne, music critic of the *Post*, "was Redford's rendition of
the aria 'Elizabeth, You Are My Woman Now.' He brought to
the song a high-pitched, whiney, nasal quality one could
hardly at first compare with the song as first performed by
Paul Robeson. But now that I ponder it, I realize that Redford's is surely as authentic an interpretation as any that
might have been imagined by the composer. More rousing
still was the jolly tune 'I Don't Have a Surfeit of Anything.' "
And so the train was set in motion, the precedent had been es-

tablished. Six months later, the Committee for the Preservation of Cultural Pluralism announced its new production of *Othello,* with Truman Capote in the role of the Moor.

But like all new cultural movements, this one also spawned a school of—well, pale imitators. For example, the main branch of the District of Columbia's public library revamped "story hour" altogether. Instead of the distinguished black actor who usually came to read from the works of Shakespeare (famous speeches usually, plus the well-known soliloquies from *Macbeth,* thereby demonstrating that the Bard belonged to all the people), actors were imported from the Old Vic company. (Sometimes students from the Royal Academy would also fly over to supplement their stipends.) And all would read in perfectly rounded tones from the works of Joel Chandler Harris, of the doings of "Frere Hare" and "Comrade Reynard" and their associates. Nor were other traditional forms of black art neglected. It cost the National Foundation on the Humanities more than three quarters of a million dollars to import the famous Boys Choir of Vienna. Its performance of the traditional spirituals in *Hochdeutsch* soprano is still the talk of the high school hockey rinks.

With such great successes, how could other spheres remain unmoved by the power of modernity? Mrs. Grently's husband, owner of a local professional sports franchise, invested heavily in an all-white basketball troupe that traveled the world in demonstration of its ball-handling proficiency. Immediately named the East Side Jetsetters, the team soon became a permanent fixture of the State Department's cultural exchange programs. Their famous warm-up session, done to the accompaniment of "Yellow Rose of Texas," has been performed in seventy-one countries and has dramatically altered the world's understanding of race relations in America, especially behind the Iron Curtain.

Meanwhile, race, color, creed, or national origin can no longer stand in the way of genuine self-expression in America. Last week a group of Mennonites in Pennsylvania petitioned the Department of State for funds to organize a traveling

Wild West Show and rodeo; a congregation of Hassidic Jews in Brooklyn has already secured funding for a combined equestrian and gymnastic expedition this fall; and the Lithuanian Community Council of Chicago will become the first ethnic group in America to stage Grand Kabuki in the authentic Japanese manner.

"I look forward to the day," commented Mrs. Grently, "when the interchangeability of minorities will have become an accomplished fact. Culture must be good for everybody, or it will be good for nobody, least of all ourselves."

Music Hath Charms

The restoration of declining American influence in the strategic Middle East has become an urgent priority. In the face of rising hostility to Western culture, the United States has decided to fall back upon its most potent weapon in the struggle for the hearts and minds of the world's peoples, namely American popular music. It has now been determined that our music has to be made both more relevant and more inspiring. A study commissioned by the Voice of America concluded that the good old tunes can still play their vital role, but only if given the appropriate flavor of the exotic Near East. Thus, the Voice of America, from its 50,000-watt, clear channel transmitter somewhere East of Suez, has begun to broadcast twenty-four hours a day.

A tabulation of postcards mailed to the station reveals that the following are now the most requested tunes:

(34) Tabriz and I
      (Sunnyat and Shariat, Pahlavi)

(33) Imama Done Told Me
      (Armed Band, Grand Mosque)

(32) Sidon, You're Rocking the Boat
      (Lebanese Luters, Atlantic)

(31) Somalia e Mobile
      (Luciano Pavorotti, American Express)

(30) I Hear Menachem, But You Can't Begin
      (Sitdown Sam and the Sinai Settlers, Jet)

(29) Hua Can I Say After Hussein You're Sorry?
      (Mojo Mao and the Gang of Four, Capitol)

(28) Amman and a Woman
      (Hareem, Epic)

(27) Oman and a Woman
      (Seraglio, OPEC)

(26) Shah na-na
      (Shah na-na, Opic)

(25) Nah, nah shah
      (Nah, nah Shah, Cipo)

(24) Sa'ana-na
      (Sa'ana-na, Aspic)

(23) Jew Eilat Up My Life
      (Jenny and the GroSingers, Tuth'piq)

(22) Just Sarkis in the Night
      (Beirut Battlers, Deutsche Gramophone Gesell-
      schaft)

(21) She Loves You Fran-ji-yeh
      (Suleiman, Wissenschaft und Gemeinschaft)

(20) I Wanna Hold Your Land
      (Sitdown Sam and the Sinai Settlers, flipside of
      ♯30)

(19) Vancing in the Dark
      (Danielle Diplomatique, Raison d'Etat)

(18) My Heart Belongs to Wadi
      (Bert Lance, BMI)

(17) My Heart Belongs to Mahdi
      (Charlton and Laurence, MCA)

(16) Born Kuwait
      (The Teddybears, Clamshell)

(15) Tutti Frutti, Baroody
      (Milton and the Nometarists, AEI)

(14) Take Djibouti
      (Par See and the Sunshine Band, BEI)

(13) If I Were a Carterer and You Were Mehedi)
      (Amuzeghur and the Sufis, CEI)

(12) Qom on Everybody
      (Eddie Cochran, Immortal)

(11) She's the Sweetheart of Zbig's Mapai
      (Stan Kurd, SRI)

(10) Apocrypha of Miracles
      (Geo. Beverly Shea, Faith)

 (9) Haifa Got Plenty of Nuthin'
      (Paul Robeson, Jr., MGM)

(8) Silva Threads and Golda Needles
    (Judy Colinsky, RCA)

(7) Dayan and Dayout
    (Genesis, Sophisticate)

(6) I Get Bahai with a Little Help from My Friends
    (Exodus, Hatha)

(5) Smack Dab in the Mitla
    (Leviticus, Riyadh)

(4) Aqaba Soul in the Bosom of Abraham
    (Isaac Hayes, Jacob, and Esau)

(3) I Feel Gidi
    (Chad and Dahomey, Vanguard)

(2) Three Times Zahedi
    (Voyager, Savak)

(1) Arish You Love
    (Pearl of the Antilles, Diamond)

Golden Oldie of the Week

Sudan Always Get What You Want
    (Qatar Slim, Atlantic)

Pick Hit of the Week

Teheran-ran-ran
    (Kemal Atatürk, Pacific)

Album of the Week

Whole Lot of Sheikin' Goin' On
    (Ibn Saud al-Assiz Memorial Orchestra and Chorus,
    CIA)

The Bookbaggers

    Having ripped the veil off the face of the film industry, having exposed the lust that lurks even in the hearts of the most respectable, having removed the smug mask of right-eousness which hides corporate reality from gullible con-sumers, America's foremost novelist was still not content. For the masterpiece of power and intrigue, the chronicle that would lay bare the ruthless struggle for power at the highest levels of government, still eluded him.

    He had come to Washington in search of material, his atta-ché case bulging with blank three-by-five cards. The city pul-sated with raw nervous energy. The presence of power was palpable. But wherever he went, the supposedly powerful bemoaned their impotence. They controlled nothing, they influenced nothing, they determined nothing. Could it be that the drama of power is an illusion, a myth without foundation?

    As he prowled the bars and the cafés, he could not learn the answer. Great things were being done, but none would say who was the mastermind behind them. The author had searched for three weeks, and one evening he confided to a bartender the depths of his disappointment.

"Over there in the corner," said the bartender, "with the three gorgeous broads, that's the centerpiece of your next work."

"You mean that mousy-looking guy with the thick-lensed glasses?" answered the writer. "You gotta be kidding me. He's the least heroic-looking guy I've ever seen. So why are those luscious-looking ladies hanging all over him?"

"Listen, friend," said the bartender, "you gotta remember what the philosopher said years ago. 'Knowledge is power.' And that man knows. He really knows."

"Who is he?" asked the author.

"The Librarian," said the bartender, "that's what we call him. Just The Librarian. Nobody ever bothers to ask his name. He just comes in, he says he's The Librarian, and the broads go crazy. He knows, you see. He knows everything, and what he doesn't know, he knows how to find out—names, dates, places, data, precedents, everything. That's the hero of your next book, believe me."

The author was intrigued. He picked up his drink and went over to the corner.

"Mind if I join you?" he asked the astigmatic one.

"Sit down, if you like," The Librarian answered, "and say hello to my lovely friends."

The author introduced himself.

"I've read all of your books," said The Librarian, "and I like your latest best of all, *The Mothkillers,* about the family that made a fortune in the camphor business. First class. Published by Rodent Press. The ISBN number was 6-517-13592-11-23; 811 pages; $17.98 retail, but $11.99 at Subsale Books. What can I do for you?"

"The barkeeper here tells me that you are the most power-ful man in Washington, that you're a natural model for the hero of my political novel," said the author.

"I do all right, I guess," said The Librarian noncommittally. "If somebody wants to know the answer, I tell him. But if I don't like him, maybe I don't tell him the answer. Maybe I tell him the book's not on the shelf, or that the computer is down, or that Biological Abstracts has no mention of the article he thinks exists. Or maybe I tell him that nobody knows what the unemployment rate was in Amarillo, Texas, in 1921. Then again, if I like somebody, I give him what he needs if what he needs is information. You see what I mean?"

"Knowledge is power," said the author.

"Now I see why you're a great author," said The Librarian. "You catch on quick."

"But most of my heroes are really macho and raunchy, real tough guys," said the author dejectedly. "How will I make use of you?"

"Not macho? Not raunchy?" said The Librarian. "There's no more vicious struggle than the one that goes on in the stacks. Let me tell you something. When I started out I was an ordinary researcher. Then I became a senior researcher. Then I became a section head. Then I became a division head. Then I became assistant to one of the Assistant Librarians, and then an Assistant Librarian. Then one of the Associate Librarians. Then Deputy Librarian. Then I finally became The Librarian."

"What happened to the man who used to be The Librarian?" asked the author.

"I murdered him," answered The Librarian. "As I had done away with all of the others who stood in my way. I murdered the Deputy Librarian by strangling him, but I made it look like the accidental tragedy of a man who had gotten his tie caught in the collator of the microfiche machine."

"Gee," said one of The Librarian's three female companions, "you sure are a man who knows what he wants."

"Shut up," said The Librarian. "If you don't shut up, it's the end of your cushy job that I fixed up for you, and it's back down to cataloguing."

"Not cataloguing again," moaned the luscious blonde. "I've

clawed my way up, and I'm never going back down to cataloguing."

"Treat me right and you'll be all right," said The Librarian. "But you're starting to bore me with those same old tricks."

The blonde shuddered.

The author was taken aback by the strange power The Librarian seemed to wield over these more than desirable females.

"Why don't you girls go powder your noses?" said The Librarian. "I've got important business here." And with that, the author began to jot down some notes in hurried fashion.

"You know," The Librarian continued, "I've had hundreds of women. I've had women from every country in the world. Whenever I feel the need for some real variety, I go down to the translation section. Tell me, author. Have you ever made it with a girl who can read medievel Samoan?"

"Not medieval Samoan," said the author, "but I once had a great time in Polynesia with a honey who knew Old Church Samoan."

"Gee," said The Librarian, "I didn't know there was anyone left who could read *that*. Let me buy you a drink!"

The drinks were served and the conversation resumed.

"How did you get started in your profession?" asked the author.

"I came up the hard way," said The Librarian. "I was the illegitimate son of an itinerant cucumber picker by a Wellesley dropout who was doing volunteer work in the Michigan cucumber fields. Shortly after I was born, my father left to pick citrus fruit, and my mother was kidnapped by a band of religious fanatics. I was raised communally by a cult that practiced the worship of Ba'al. But I always did well on standardized tests, and I won a scholarship to Phillips Andover Academy. I enrolled in college, but I left school after a tragic love affair my junior year."

"What happened?" interrupted the author.

"My girlfriend was unfaithful to me, so I poisoned her," said The Librarian. "But I made it look like an accident."

The author took another note.

"I drifted aimlessly for a while," continued The Librarian, "but I couldn't find myself. I had no sense of purpose. Finally, it came to me. I decided to re-enter the university and to study for the degree of Master of Library Science. I graduated first in my class, and I came here to work in The Library."

"I have to admit," said the author, "that this is the stuff of great fiction."

"From the beginning," The Librarian resumed, "everybody could see that I was pretty tough. Bogie the Bibliographer, they called me. But always behind my back, never to my face. When I became Deputy Librarian, I really began to build the network of information suppliers that has given me a stranglehold over the government. I destroyed the President's re-election campaign by supplying false information on the decline of fish imports during his first term. Actually, they had gone up, you see. And I had to do in the Chief Justice when I found out that his clerks were doing research in their library, not in The Library. Then I computerized everything so that nobody could find out anything without first coming to me. Then I switched the programs without telling anyone, and for a month nobody could find out anything. I relented only after the rich and the powerful started to give me expensive presents and large cash payments. Now, if somebody crosses me, I just shut him out. Let me say, controlling access to the stacks is like having money in the Information Bank," chuckled The Librarian.

"I didn't realize," said the author, "that a librarian could be a man to reckon with."

"Let me tell you something," said The Librarian. "When I first started out as a junior researcher, I was befriended by a crusty old man who worked in serials. He told me something I've never forgotten. In the information sector, there are two kinds of people—the givers and the takers. If you just give and let them take, they'll walk all over you. They'll stomp you into the ground. They'll scratch your eyes out. They'll drain your memory core dry, and then they'll cast you aside like an old piece of magnetic tape. They'll take your terminal if you let them. In short, they'll byte your head off."

The author was impressed. Almost immediately, the project took shape in his mind. Others had written of hotels and airports and bus stations. But here was a conception worthy of his talents. Perhaps he would call it, simply, *Library*. But he knew that he would have to come up with a racier title.

By this time the young ladies had returned. "I've got to turn in early tonight," said The Librarian. "Tomorrow I'm off for Europe to see my friends at the British Museum Library, La Bibliothèque in Paris, Die Bibliothek in Berlin, and a few other places. Then I have to show up in Brussels for a meeting of the NATO librarians, so we can coordinate strategy."

"What about us?" asked one of the females seductively.

"Not tonight, sugar," replied The Librarian casually. "After all, I've got to pay attention to our bread and butter. Take our friend here, the author. Where would he be if people didn't get into bed with a good book every once in a while?"

The Moving Picture Writes

The first Hollywood production company with the savvy to take an option on this scenario for the first great disaster film with a political motif is going to rake in big bucks. And here it is:

The impossible has finally happened. The huge 747 carrying the network crews has gone down somewhere over the Pacific. The trip had been uneventful, the predictable live coverage of the President's monthly trip to Peking, routine business, like weekends in Camp David. But the plane is down; the market is down; the price of gold is up. The presidents of the three major networks issue a joint appeal to listeners to pray for their favorite anchorperson. They have not given up hope. Promotions are not announced.

The scene shifts to the Pacific itself. It happens that life rafts were not provided for the technical personnel. They perish. The broadcasters, however, climb aboard self-inflating rafts. They drift for days. They have plenty of water, but their food gives out. They contemplate cannibalism. But in what order should the survivors be consumed? Someone proposes that Tom Brokaw be the first to be eaten, because he is so handsome. Someone who has spent time as a correspondent in Paris comes up with an elaborate recipe for Brokaw.

The scene shifts. We zoom in on Eric Sevareid and Howard K. Smith, who, as we expect, are in a raft of their own. Out of respect for these two sages, the others solicit their opinion. They save Brokaw by stating that they will refuse a serving of Brokaw, even if it is offered. They find the mere suggestion unnerving. It says things about the human race which can be construed as unflattering to the species. They return to their own discussion. It deals with modern translations of the *Iliad*. Sevareid, even though he has a greater reputation for liberalism, prefers the older work of Richmond Lattimore. Smith prefers the more recent effort of Robert Fitzgerald. But they agree that the contemplation of cannibalism is balanced by the willingness of men to undertake new translations of the *Iliad*.

The scene shifts. We zoom in on another raft, where unspeakable things are happening. They involve the male and female broadcasters. If you want to find out about them, you'll have to see the movie.

The scene shifts. Sevareid and Smith continue their musings. They have now been adrift for eighteen days. All of Sevareid's hairs are still perfectly in place. His suit is unwrinkled. He is not suffering from sunburn. Smith is in equally good shape. They speculate that there is something lacking in their younger colleagues; maybe they lack staying power; they certainly look disheveled. They put this aside and resume their earlier discussion. Appropriately enough, they are discussing the Law of the Sea. Smith knows a surprising amount about the manganese nodules that rest on the ocean floor. Sevareid, who had begun with a position sympathetic to that of the Third World, comes closer to Smith's position that the deep seas should remain open to mining by commercial enterprises.

They are pleased that they have reached a consensus on this thorny issue. They agree that they will relay it personally to the Secretary of State upon their return. Sevareid discovers among his belongings a copy of the *I Ching* in the original Chinese. He begins work on a translation of it. Smith does some more work on an especially difficult double-crostic sent to him by Elliot Richardson.

The scene shifts. We zoom in on the three anchormen— Cronkite, Chancellor, and Reynolds. John and Walter agree they should dispose of Frank, but can't think of a way to do it, now that Eric and Howard have ruled out devouring him. They argue among themselves about the effect on the world should one or another of them expire. John and Frank agree that the loss of Walter would be the most keenly felt.

The scene shifts. It turns out that Howard has an interest in the natural sciences that had hitherto gone unsuspected. He holds Eric spellbound with a discussion of recent developments in cosmological theory. Howard explains the difference between a black hole and a white dwarf. Eric counters with a racy, though unprintable, joke. Eric agrees that astrophysics can be a source of new philosophical insights. They glance over at the anchormen, who have resumed their argument. Eric and Howard agree that there is a certain elemental toughness in the anchormen, even if the anchormen lack grounding in the Western humanistic tradition that produces the more interesting commentary.

The scene shifts. After drifting helplessly for twenty-seven days, the survivors are taken aboard a North Korean fishing boat. They sail to North Korea. They are taken to Pyongyang. Negotiations begin. One month later, the Pyongyang government announces that the five men have signed to do the evening news on Pyongyang TV. The world does not know whether they are doing it under duress, or for money. All we know is that ratings soar. Meanwhile, Barbara Walters arrives and films an exclusive interview with the great leader of the Korean people, the ever-victorious iron-willed supreme commander Marshal Kim Il Sung. Marshal Kim cannot speak

English and Barbara cannot speak Korean, so the interview is conducted in Finnish, which both of them speak fluently.

Six months pass. The latest ratings are released and they show that the number of Koreans watching the evening news in its new format has declined slightly. Three more months pass, and the new ratings show that the number of viewers is down sharply. This makes Marshal Kim very angry. He meets with his board, and they decide that they will no longer pay these astronomical sums if the three anchormen and the two commentators cannot produce a growing audience. Marshal Kim fires all five of them. The broadcasters return to America. Walter is relieved to discover that, even during all those months, Mudd has *still* not been promoted to anchorman. Everybody goes back to his old job, except Eric. He resigns. He is appointed Regius Professor of Modern History at Oxford University.

Truth in Packaging

One of the great victories for the American tradition of plain old common sense was the establishment of the Federal Religion Commission. Many groups claimed credit for its creation, but the honor quite obviously belongs to a broad coalition of consumer advocates. It had been understood for a long while that religion was the largest unregulated industry in America. Even the oil companies contributed more in taxes to the Federal Treasury than did the various Multinational Religious Combines (a fact which, in itself, was thought miraculous by some). Religion as a whole had sustained a real growth rate of more than 5 percent per annum and, by the end of the most recent decade, it had become the largest single industry in America. Even though it was a service industry, it accounted for more than 40 percent of the Gross National Product.

The first question the consumer lobby had to address was

whether these trends resulted from the worship of God or Mammon. Obviously, earnings derived from the worship of Mammon ought to be taxed at the usual corporate rate. Various studies were adduced to prove that Mammon dominated at least 60 percent of the religious sector, and was on the verge of acquiring a monopoly. Antitrust action would then be in order. But that portion of the market still controlled by God was a totally different matter. In truth—and this had been known for millennia—it was difficult to tell whether it was God or Mammon who was being worshipped.

The second problem was of a more traditional sort. With the proliferation of new religious brand names, large advertising claims were being made. New religions were constantly being test-marketed. Existing federal regulations require the purveyors to list all the ingredients contained therein, but there was no enforcement mechanism sufficient to the task. By the time federal investigators had managed to evaluate the claims of fraud that had been filed, it happened more often than not that the marketer had gone out of business, declared bankruptcy, or disappeared as a result of a merger with, or an acquisition by, a larger concern. This had been the case, for example, when New Age Transcendental Cult, Inc., had made a tender offer for all the outstanding shares of Black Hills Spirits Worshipping Company. Many investors were wiped out.

Some order had to be brought out of the chaos that reigned in the marketplace of religious ideas. This was the ultimate test of political science and administrative theory. To argue that they were no match for theology was to admit defeat in the great experiment at self-government, for government was the largest source of financial support for the pursuit of truth in areas as diverse as economics and subatomic physics. A coordinated federal effort, as great as the Manhattan Project or the Apollo Project, had to be launched. The President himself had committed the nation to that great goal. He had called for a mobilization of the best minds in America to win the battle against uncertainty. "We will know the unknowable before the end of the decade," the President had pledged.

So the Federal Religion Commission should be seen as an interim measure, designed to go out of business as soon as the nation establishes its theological independence. But this has not prevented the Commission from pursuing its responsibilities, pursuant to the Truth in Religion Act which created it.

The first case brought before the Commission concerned the oldest of the monotheistic creeds, Judaism. It had been alleged that the Jews had been claiming that they were the chosen people, but that there was insufficient evidence for this claim. The petitioners, therefore, requested the Commission to issue a cease-and-desist order forthwith. Briefs were submitted and testimony was taken. But the Commission, by a 6–3 vote, ruled against the petitioners on the grounds that the Jews had never claimed that they had been chosen for anything in particular, only that they were chosen as such, and that the weight of the evidence suggested that they had indeed been chosen for something or other. The petitioners erred, the majority of the Commission argued, by assuming that the claim to be "chosen" implied "chosen for something better than that others get chosen for." Yet, as everyone knew, the lot of the Jews throughout history implied that they might have been chosen for something else. Thus, the claim to be the "chosen people" was governed by the prior principle of "caveat emptor." Anyone who decided to become a Jew on this basis would find out about it sooner or later.

Six months later, a coalition called the Arrogance of Power Defense Fund brought a class-action suit against thirty-eight Christian sects, alleging that their claim that "the meek shall inherit the earth" was patently false and misleading. The coalition's suit attempted to break new legal ground by arguing that the assertion "the meek shall inherit the earth" should be banned on the grounds that it was obscene. "The proposition," the petitioners claimed, "meets the criteria established by the Supreme Court itself regarding obscenity and pornography, to wit, the assertion in question is 'utterly without redeeming social value.' Anyone with even half a brain knows that this assertion about the meek violates every accepted norm and all community standards. No locality in America accepts such a proposition. It is *prima facie* absurd. Talk about the meek inheriting the earth! They haven't inherited a single town council in the Republic."

This was a novel argument indeed. To apply the test of "redeeming social value" was to open up an enormous can of worms. It soon became apparent that, by this standard, practically everything would have to be banned, confiscated, and burned. Surely, this was not what the Supreme Court had intended. Or was it? The Commission put off the case until the following year.

The Federal Reserve Board also brought a case before the Commission. Acting in its capacity as the nation's central bank, the Board sought restraining orders against two Islamic sects in St. Louis which had opened a bank. The bank operated in strict accordance with the ancient Koranic principle that usury was immoral. Therefore, the bank lent money but charged no interest whatsoever. At first, the Comptroller of the Currency had been reluctant to issue a charter to the First National Islamic Bank of St. Louis, noting that it was certain that the bank would fail. But after five years of operation, the bank was firmly in the black; in fact, even though it charged no interest for loans, it was phenomenally profitable nonetheless. The Federal Reserve Board was much interested in this. The bank itself refused to answer question ⌗39 on the Federal Reserve's R-L form, claiming that the query "How in God's name is it possible for your bank to make money without charging interest?" violated the bank's protections under the First and Fifth Amendments. "None of your god damn business" had been the reply, if the truth be told.

The Federal Religion Commission was asked to order the officers of the bank to enroll in an introductory economics course at the University of Missouri. "The notion that banks can lend money at no interest, yet still turn a profit, threatens the entire financial structure of the nation," the Federal Reserve Board had maintained in its complaint. "The Board of Directors of this financial institution should not only be ordered to cease and desist, the Directors should be re-educated. And if they refuse to be re-educated, they should be deported." However, this case was also postponed for one year, and all nine of the Commissioners took advantage of the opportunity to contract for no-cost auto loans at the Islamic Bank.

The Coalition of Concerned Conservative Parents, a neighborhood group in Washington, D.C., filed a complaint against their local Methodist church for stressing, in Sunday school, the phrase ". . . and a little child shall lead them." The Infants' Defense Fund filed a counterbrief, maintaining that the proposition was "self-evident." The IDF's lawyer maintained further, during an administrative hearing, that "the choice before this Commission is clear. Either it affirms the thoroughly discredited doctrine of *in loco parentis,* or it affirms the theological underpinning of the libertarian thesis that children should not only be allowed to do more or less what they want to do, but that leadership positions in this society should be opened to them in accordance with their percentage of the population." The Commission declined to hear this case, on the grounds that it probably had something to do with affirmative action. It was referred to the Justice Department.

Now, so far as the religious groups were concerned, the activities of the Federal Religion Commission were nothing but an enormous bother. No one anticipated the ingenious counterattack they would launch, for, instead of seeking to restrict the applicability of the Truth in Religion Act, they sought to expand it. The idea was disarmingly simple. The greater the number of groups that could be brought under the act's purview, the larger the number of people who would become interested in doing away with it. Accordingly, it was necessary to redefine as religious activity that which was formerly thought to be "mere commerce."

In accordance with this stratagem, the Committee for the Exercise of Unregulated Religion filed a complaint before the Commission, alleging that the cosmetics industry was a religious sect subject to Commission control. "The cosmetics industry is a religious enterprise," they maintained. "It is based on the Revlon creed, the doctrine that holds that outer beauty has nothing to do with the beauty of the inner soul." The complainants elaborated on this theme, charging somewhat later that life insurance was also a religion. "Indeed," they argued, "the basic premise of the life insurance industry, namely, that the future is now, is a theological concept. The economic basis of the industry—pay premiums now, derive benefits later—is nothing but the operational consequence of the ancient maxim that the Lord giveth and the Lord taketh away." (The same, they said, held true for the airline industry, for "air travel was the functional equivalent of an invitation to put one's faith in God.") These cases produced nothing but the worst sort of legal pettifoggery—the lawyers for the insurers arguing that "own a piece of the rock" referred to the Rock of Gibraltar, their opponents arguing that the phrase quite clearly connoted the Rock of Ages.

It was quite startling that the Federal Religion Commission, quite unlike the run-of-the-mill federal agency, did not take advantage of this opportunity to expand its jurisdiction into nearly all aspects of American life. "These cases," the Commission held, "would require us to delve into the fundamental legitimacy of the Republic itself. This we are not competent to judge."

The Commissioners were quite right. A group of agnostics asked the Commission to rule on the veracity of the national motto "In God We Trust." Five veterans' organizations meanwhile argued the case for "Trust in God, but keep your powder dry." But the Commission refused to be drawn into dogmatism. "Congress gave us a mandate for skepticism," the Commission pronounced, "and Congress would surely abolish us if we were to enjoin even the Military-Industrial Complex from completing its appointed rounds: Praise the Lord and pass the ammunition."

The Old Curiosity Shop

Collectors of political mementos, old curios, Washington memorabilia, used campaign buttons, rare first editions of government documents, snatches of audio- and videotape, have established the Old Curiosity Shop as their Mecca. Preston Lapschul, the shop's proprietor, tours the country for these valuable historical artifacts and is often seen rummaging through piles of castoffs, looking for that one intriguing item which can illuminate an entire era in our history. (It was Lapschul, for example, who unearthed the oldest extant memo from a campaign manager to his candidate. The memorandum urges then-candidate James Madison to run as Jimmy Madison, a simple Virginia farmer, rather than as James Madison, Father of the Constitution. The anti-Washington mood can thus be traced well back into the early nineteenth century. But the same consulting firm had better luck with Jimmy Monroe, convincing him to run as plain James. Lapschul himself attributes the assassination of James Garfield to his failure to campaign as Jimmy Garfield. ("A stuffy name like James was bound to arouse the ire of a disappointed office seeker," Lapschul says.)

Lapschul also has a large collection of old photographs. He offers a daguerreotype of Chester A. Arthur's first Cabinet. He has a photograph of Dwight Eisenhower's Postmaster General, Arthur Summerfield, shaking hands with the letter carrier of the year. He has a Xerox copy of a memorandum to Lyndon B. Johnson suggesting that he campaign as good ole Lindy. He has an original, not a facsimile, of the printed program when Thomas Jefferson himself spoke at the first annual dinner of the Anti-Federalist Congressional Campaign Committee. He has the only complete set of bumper stickers for all three Wallace Presidential campaigns—Henry, George, and Irving.

Students of the inner history of government regulation will find a handwritten draft of the first set of regulations ever issued by the Civil Aeronautics Board, allowing for the serving of alcoholic beverages on transcontinental flights. One will also find a set of drawings made by the five finalists in the most important competition ever run by the federal government—selecting the design and the wording of the best-known of government mottos—"Warning: The Surgeon General Has Determined That Cigarette Smoking Is Dangerous to Your Health." (The runner-up was DANGER: THE SURGEON GENERAL WARNS YOU THAT YOUR HEALTH IS IN JEOPARDY FROM THE SMOKING OF CIGARETTES.)

There is also much that will catch the eye of the aficionado of American diplomatic history. It was Lapschul who shed new light on Admiral Dewey's famous naval victory at Manila Bay during the Spanish-American War. In an "eyes only" message for President McKinley, Dewey had written, "We have met the enemy, and he's for sale." Lapschul also unearthed a hitherto lost note from Mrs. Woodrow Wilson to her husband, the President. In the note, Mrs. Wilson calls her husband a "dumb son of a bitch" for allowing the country to get sucked into World War I. Lapschul also has materials which finally resolve the controversy over the relationship between President Jefferson and Sally Hemmings. It turns out that they were just good friends after all.

So far as social history is concerned, Lapschul's assiduous searches allow us to understand the ferocity with which the new federal government suppressed Shays's Rebellion in 1786. Apparently, a stenographic error in the message sent to the Secretary of War described the episode as "Gays' Rebellion," causing the Secretary, a man renowned for his intolerance, to order the massacre of the rebels. This has never been forgiven in some parts of the country. Likewise, we are now able to unravel the curious set of circumstances which led to the passage of the Volstead Act, the law which provided the enforcement mechanism for the failed experiment in Prohibition. The act barely passed. It seems that the deciding vote was cast by Senator Zebulon Trevell of Colorado. His newly discovered diary records that he became very angry with the brewing industry. Trevell recounts that he was minding his own business at a cocktail party, when he was almost trampled to death by the Schlitz Malt Liquor Bull.

Lapschul also possesses the first set of pornographic etchings run off in secret by the night crew at the Government Printing Office. Lapschul explains to all who will listen that this was but the tip of the iceberg. The Superintendent of Documents, the man to whom conscientious Americans send twenty-five cents in coin in order to receive the latest government pamphlet on the proper method for preserving old dinosaur bones, was at the heart of a nationwide ring of smut peddlers. His role came to light, quite by accident, in 1931. A retired schoolmarm in Idaho turned him in when, instead of receiving a tulip bulb planting schedule in her self-addressed return envelope, she received a pirated edition of *Lady Chatterley's Lover*. The scandal was hushed up for more than forty years.

But it is the technological revolution which makes the modern age what it is. More often than not, important business is now conducted by telephone, not by written correspondence, and it is often difficult to collect and frame telephone calls. Lapschul has solved this problem by stocking the largest set of wiretap transcripts ever assembled. He has had the transcripts reproduced and attractively bound in impressive-looking volumes. They are unedited. His arrangement with the History of These United States Book Club has been very lucrative. It is now possible to own not merely the *Collected Correspondence of Warren G. Harding* in four volumes but also eleven volumes of *Selected Telephonic Communications of President Warren G. Harding.* (They are available at a cost of one dollar for the set if the subscriber agrees to purchase the telephonic communications of three Secretaries of the Interior.) In a major coup, Lapschul also acquired the complete record collection of President Calvin Coolidge, which is now available on synthetic stereo as *A Connoisseur's Guide to the Jazz Age.*

None of this should be taken to suggest that Lapschul is a man out for the quick buck. People are welcome to come into his shop and just browse, knowing that the highest standards of ethics will be maintained by the proprietor. His competitors, after all, operate nothing but tourist traps. Like the midwestern tourists who have purchased the Brooklyn Bridge, more than one Washington visitor has been suckered into buying what some salesman assures him is *the* missing eighteen-and-a-half-minute tape segment.

"That's the sort of thing," observes Lapschul, "which gives all of us in this business a bad name."

Fiction

Ezra Platt Lincoln, an employee of the Department of Agriculture, had temporarily retired on the proceeds of his best-selling Washington novel. His book was a teeth-clenching thriller about a resourceful investigator from the Soil Conservation Service who managed to arrest the spreading wheat blight which threatened the world's supply of Wonder Bread. The film version had been a commercial blockbuster, an enormous stimulus to paperback sales. Whole shopping centers were set ablaze by enraged children and panicked mothers as the nation's store of Wonder Bread began gradually to decline. Not even the personal assurances of the President that the blight would eventually be eliminated could stem the tide of mass hysteria. Before the Soil Conservation Service brought matters under control, the price of a loaf of Wonder Bread had soared to eleven dollars a loaf—when you could get it at all.

Mr. Lincoln, grown fabulously rich, went off to a mountain retreat, with a Delphic promise that a sequel would soon be forthcoming—involving the same hero—this time concerning his efforts to isolate the pernicious bacillus that was slowly destroying the nation's reserves of creamy peanut butter.

Lincoln thus became a living hero to federal bureaucrats of literary bent. His picture began to appear throughout federal office buildings, providing inspiration to those who sought fulfillment through creativity. The Washington novel, previously the preserve of journalists and convicted felons, was taken over by the people who knew Washington best, the men and women who made it work, the indefatigable soldiers on the front line of administrative law and procedure.

Now here was a vast reservoir of creative energy with enormous financial potential. Properly organized, it could become the basis of a new, vertically integrated industry. All that remained was the arrival of a single-minded visionary genius who could take hold of that inchoate possibility and mold it into a potent cultural and economic force. Ironically, it was Ezra Platt Lincoln himself who grasped the fact that assembly-line techniques could be applied to the writing and publishing of Washington novels. No longer would the industry be the domain of widely scattered individual entrepreneurs working in isolation. Rather, under Lincoln's direction, they would be brought together in a single place and welded into a disciplined labor force, with all the economies of scale that would inevitably result.

The first step was the incorporation of Lincoln's holding company, Amalgamated Political Fiction. Through a series of intricate financial maneuvers and brilliantly executed futures trades in the New York Literary Exchange, Lincoln secured exclusive rights to all patents and formulas concerning Washington novels. He established his factory in a nearby suburb, and began a massive advertising campaign to recruit a proper labor force. Just as at the dawn of the Industrial Revolution in eighteenth-century England, the initial work force was composed of women. They were drawn to Lincoln's mill by the prospect of cash earnings. Lincoln had suspected that the labor pool was enormous, for there were, throughout the Washington metropolitan area, wives of bureaucrats, elected officials, and untenured professors who had been working away on novels—but to little effect. Indeed, anyone who was anyone had a wife hard at work on a potential best seller.

Such writers could, under Lincoln's scheme, become indentured novelists. The scheme was elegantly simple. In return for signing over the rights to the unique idea contained in their individual efforts, Lincoln provided a work space, paper, correcto-type, a typewriter, and sharpened pencils—and a guarantee that he would pay 25¢ for each complete page of manuscript. Thus, the income to be derived from each individual project—and who did not think that income would be so derived?—was available immediately, rather than being deferred until some vague date in the future. And the piece-rate system Lincoln employed was the best sort of motivation. By turning out ten acceptable pages of copy a day, the women of Washington could return home with an additional $2.50. And since Lincoln always paid in cash at the end of a day's work well done, there were no problems of taxation and withholding and health insurance. For each writer was signed on as an independent contractor, leaving the Internal Revenue Service to scratch its head over the tax-shelter implications of the scheme. Moreover, Lincoln insisted on a five-day work-week, so that weekends were free for his workers to discuss the week's progress when they gathered at their tennis clubs over the weekend. No more the courtside complaints about writer's block!

In fact, Lincoln's Washington novel factory was a show-place of efficiency and quickly established a certain notoriety. The work was done at long tables, each seventy-five feet in length and about five feet wide. Typewriters were placed at two-foot intervals, and the writers were seated on metal folding chairs. Large racks of paper were strung over-head, and finished copy was retrieved by a corps of pre-teenage children—most of them belonging to the workers—who ran to pick up each completed page after its author rang a bell. The pages were neatly filed by the number of each writer in large bins. At the end of the day, clerks tallied the output and paid the wages.

The din was deafening. As an energy-conservation measure, Lincoln provided mechanical typewriters only. Between the clanging of typewriters and the ringing of bells, the noise could become quite overwhelming. Every so often, there would be a hideous industrial accident, for pieces of hair and clothing were forever being tangled up in the typewriters. At such times, the bodily injuries could be horrible to behold, but not even the stench of blood or the heartrending cries of pain halted production. Brutality and efficiency were the essence of the system, and repeated visits by representatives of the Occupational Safety and Health Administration failed to bring about any amelioration in working conditions. For the fact was that the bureaucrats who ran OSHA had more than their share of wives and girlfriends at work in Lincoln's literary factory, and they were not about to close it down because of an occasional broken fingernail or smashed pinky.

As his labor force expanded, Lincoln required ever larger quantities of raw materials. Each day, large vans would arrive at his freight dock and enormous crates of government documents would be unloaded. These Lincoln had purchased at federal surplus sales—usually the ancient records of some obscure government agency, records which would have otherwise been sold as waste paper and reduced to pulp. But under Lincoln's direction, the papers were spread out at worktables, and children from the inner city were given gainful employment by arranging them in neat piles, cutting out every paragraph, such that the documents would tell an exciting story of their own.

In this manner, the papers of the Federal Meteorological Service of the late 1930's were fashioned into a thrilling tale of how polyethylene came to replace natural rubber in the construction of weather balloons. The old archives of the Bureau of Fisheries Management became an exciting novel of one man's struggle to have fishnet manufactured from nylon, rather than string, and how vast fortunes accumulated in the making of string fishnets were wiped out by the bone-crushing onslaught of modern technology. Turn-of-the-century papers of the Office of Marine Mammalian Species told a shocking tale—surely shocking to the modern sensibility—of how the federal government actually encouraged and subsidized the harpooning of whales and the clubbing of infant seals! The nation, upon reading even the fictionalized account produced by Lincoln's factory, was appropriately incensed. Somehow, Lincoln acquired the old records of the now defunct Selective Service System, dating from the early 1920's, especially those detailing every disqualification for military service related to alleged homosexuality. There were no names, of course, every individual being identified solely by an eight-digit number. Still, small communities were shocked to discover what some of their inhabitants—especially the notorious ⚹387-91-189 of Muncie, Indiana—had been up to in 1922.

From writing table to press to bookshop to mail-order book club, Lincoln's Amalgamated Political Fiction soon acquired a dominant position in the writing and marketing of Washington novels. Smaller competitors were ruthlessly run out of business. Aspiring novelists, who thought they had a wholly original plot, were routinely beaten into print by Amalgamated Political Fiction. Within the publishing industry itself, APF was known simply as the "octopus," its tentacles slowly reaching even into foreign capitals where labor was cheaper and government papers even more readily accessible. Thus the London novel, the Paris novel, the Rome novel, the Seoul novel, all came to be mass-produced. Lincoln himself journeyed personally to both Peking and Moscow and established, in both places, writers' collectives which produced the first novels of bureaucratic intrigue within the Kremlin and the Forbidden City. All were immediate best sellers on five continents.

In less than five years, it became possible to think of Amalgamated Political Fiction as a trust, then as an international cartel. Even as Lincoln aspired to a true global monopoly on the sale of contemporary political fiction, the fundamental laws of economics eventually overtook his Faustian ambitions. For supply soon began to overrun demand. Even the establishment of a mail-order book club in China ("If every Chinese read only two political thrillers a month, we could sell twenty-four billion copies a year in China alone!" Lincoln had once exclaimed) could not cope with the exponential growth in supply. And so Lincoln's dreams of a political novel cartel were dashed. In fact, the market for his books collapsed altogether in 1993, when something akin to an epidemic swept the Western Hemisphere; people were getting sick of such works, and then sick from them.

Lincoln, to be sure, had made his fortune. Like the Standard Oil Trust, his endeavors gave economic historians something to write about, for it was a unique period in the history of literature *and* of high finance. And, like the original John D. Rockefeller, he lived on well into his nineties; but instead of handing out dimes, he would hand out free paperback copies of his own latest novelistic endeavor.

Ezra Platt Lincoln died in Lawrence, Kansas, in the heart of the wheat-growing country that had produced the theme for his first commerical success. On his desk was the half-completed manuscript he had been working on—about the first test-tube baby to become the first transsexual President of the United States.

The Highest Bidder

For the children of the rich, the wellborn, or merely the upwardly mobile nouveau riche, the citizens of Washington maintain an excellent system of private schools. (These institutions cater to every educational need; indeed, Washington is the site of the nation's premier school for children with learning disabilities, namely, Phillips Dyslexeter Academy.) But inflation has taken its toll, and even the best-endowed of these schoolhouses must engage in the public solicitation of funds. Distinguished citizens contribute of their time and substance; all are willing to participate in the Annual Auction, where their contributions are auctioned off to the highest bidder. The Capital is an ideal site for such activity, for that which can be offered is interesting and varied, and the Annual Auction never fails to exceed even the most optimistic expectations of the fund raisers.

Last week, at a sectarian school of great eminence, the bidding was hot and heavy. The Director of the National Institute of Mental Health contributed two years of psychoanalysis (four days per week). The bidding reached a high of $31,000, until it was realized that government employees, by virtue of their health insurance, receive free psychiatric care, whereupon all bids were withdrawn.

A senior partner in Washington's best-known law firm offered a one-year lobbying effort to secure passage of any one piece of legislation in the Congress. The contest shook down to a test of wills and financial nerve between a prominent car dealer, who wanted the repeal of all federal emission-control standards, and an eccentric millionaire, who wanted a moratorium on the construction of new buildings in the District of Columbia. The car dealer offered the winning bid of $475,000, a bargain for both the school and the dealer. Such services are seldom had for less than three quarters of a million.

The director of the National Institute of Pathology offered an autopsy, to be performed on the corpse of the high bidder's choice. The winning bid was tendered by Trenton Dougland, Special Counsel to the Coalition Against Cover-up of Conspiracy, which, convinced that President Benjamin Harrison did not die of natural causes, wished to have his body exhumed and examined for evidence of foul play. Dougland himself theorized that Harrison's death was the work of the Jesuits.

A professor of anthropology offered two free tickets to his next public lecture on sociobiology, which elicited a high bid of seventy-one cents.

The conductor of the National Sympathy Orchestra offered the first chair in the violin section for one evening to an aspiring violinist. The winning bid of $11,400 was tendered by Mrs. Nathan Fishbein, whose eight-year-old grandson, Jascha, was doing splendidly in his Suzuki violin class. Mrs. Fishbein also announced a matching gift to the school's program in musical education.

The commander of the Strategic Air Command offered a nuclear strike, to be directed against the target of the high bidder's choice. The high bidder was Washington's richest orthopedic surgeon, a socially prominent physician and a well-known patron of the arts. For $185,000 the physician secured the destruction of Cranford, Ohio, thereby obliterating all trace of his humble social origins, and ensuring that no one who "knew him when" would be able to talk.

The Secretary of State offered a seat on his airplane for his next round of "shuttle diplomacy" between South Africa and Black Africa. The winning bid of $668—only slightly below the group rate, night coach, no-more-than-eighteen-nor-fewer-than-twenty-one-days,* regular tourist-class fare—was submitted by Jacques Aupierre. Monsieur Aupierre, fabulously rich, had once been an abjectly poor Creole immigrant from Haiti. At the age of seventy-three, he wanted to do something to promote a reconciliation between the races before he died.

The manager of Field Investigations of the Federal Bureau of Investigation offered to find out everything anyone could possibly want to know about one individual of the high bidder's choice. The winning bid was submitted by Roger Artlow, an insomniac hopelessly addicted to Washington's most popular late-night radio call-in show. Mr. Artlow wanted to know what the host of the show really looked like.

Washington's best-known madam offered twenty-four hours of diversion at her establishment. After some discussion, it was decided that this item had to be auctioned off with sealed bids. The high bidder was not announced.

The State Party Committee of an adjoining state offered its nomination for the office of United States senator. The Senate seat was snapped up for a cool four and a half million dollars by a socially prominent widow, who thereupon gave it to her unemployed nephew.

The best-known divorce lawyer in the city offered his services, gratis, in any child-custody battle of the high bidder's choice. The winning bid was submitted by José Rafael Mayagüez, exiled dictator of a South American country. Señor Mayagüez was involved in a complex legal tangle with the

---

* Pending approval of the Civil Aeronautics Board (CAB).

revolutionaries who had overthrown him; they wanted custody of his oldest son in order to execute him.

The president of Washington's largest publishing house offered to publish any previously unpublished manuscript of the high bidder's choice. The highest bid of $691 was submitted by Cao Buu Huu, formerly *chargé d'affaires* at the South Vietnamese Embassy. The manuscript turned out to be the long-lost love letters that had been sent by Nguyen Van Thieu to a well-known American folk singer.

Not to be outdone by a publishing company, the managing editor of the newspaper with the greatest circulation in the Washington metropolitan area agreed to distribute a special Sunday supplement of the high bidder's own choosing. The successful bidder was a small company which specialized in the making of hammocks. The supplement, of which almost 900,000 copies were later distributed, made a pitch for the firm's most exotic product—an electrically wired hammock which could send sensuous charges of electricity into the body of anyone stretched out in it.

Finally, the evening closed with the customary offer from the Committee for the Re-Nomination, Re-Election, and Re-Inauguration of the President—the Vice-Presidency. The bidding continues.

Movie Review

The Redemption of Bo Glynnan and Other Films

Reviewed by Rowena Harband

Since the death of my late husband, Congressman Franklin Harband, the Washington *Press* has been generous to a fault in hiring me as its reviewer of political fiction with a Washington motif. I am a little nervous about venturing into film criticism, but the editors here have been very encouraging. In the first place, our regular film critic has been awarded a Nieman Fellowship at Harvard, where he will study the impact of the works of Ingmar Bergman on photojournalism. And besides, there is a big bunch of new movies about our town and, for a change, they portray you and me and all our friends in a better light than we have been used to getting from Hollywood. I know this is true because all the movies I have been instructed to review are rated G.

The first movie I want to talk about is *The Redemption of Bo Glynnan*. It's very realistic and well acted. The hero, Bo Glynnan, is a small-town politician from a mountainous region. He is a real scoundrel. He drinks a lot, is unfaithful to his wife, and gambles excessively. What's more, he is totally corrupt. He makes it very plain that if he is elected to the Senate, he is going to sell his vote to the highest bidder.

But when Bo gets to Washington, he undergoes a complete metamorphosis. He realizes that political power provides a chance to do good and to work hard. He stops drinking, gives up gambling, and becomes an exemplary family man. He applies himself diligently. The climax of the movie occurs when he secures passage of a bill which improves life for millions of people. In the final fade-out, shot on the White House lawn, we see Senator Glynnan receiving the pen the President has used to sign this bill into law. This movie is very good because it points out the positive effects fame and power can have on the development of individual character.

Another good movie is *Mr. Smith Goes to Chevy Chase*. This is a remake of a classic of the 1940's. In this version, the son of the original Mr. Smith also goes to Washington to fight the corrupt interests and to serve the people. But he finds that, because of his father's good work, the people are being well served and that there is little, if any, corruption. He decides that he wishes to live in the same house his father lived in when he was in Washington. But when he gets to the house, he finds out that the neighborhood has changed, so he decides to move to Chevy Chase, a nearby suburb. He lives there for eighteen months, and finally decides to go home and tell the people that the government really is in good hands and they have nothing to worry about.

One film I really liked is called *The Night of the Corporals*. This movie tells the story of three Army corporals stationed at a fort close to Washington who decide to go into the city for a day. They take the bus. They tour all the historic places and

also find time to take in a museum. After dinner, they go to a
concert of the National Symphony Orchestra, where they
meet three young coeds from a local junior college. They invite the coeds to have ice cream with them. The six of them
all go to an ice-cream parlor, where they have banana splits
and hot fudge sundaes. But the corporals realize that it is almost 11:30 P.M. and that they must therefore return to their
base immediately. They take the telephone numbers of the
coeds and promise they will call soon. The corporals go to the
bus station and the coeds return to their dormitory. They look
forward to seeing each other again because everybody thinks
everyone is friendly and nice.

If you enjoy spine-tingling suspense in a movie, I recommend *The Night of the Colonels*. In this movie, four Army
colonels, who have become disenchanted with the way things
are going in the country, decide that they will conspire together and pull off a military coup. To learn more about the
government they are plotting to overthrow, they go to the library and read a copy of the *Federalist Papers*. After they
read it, they realize that a military coup would be unconstitutional, so they decide to work through the system. They
encourage their wives to join the local chapter of the League
of Women Voters, and they begin to participate actively in
local and neighborhood affairs. The ringleader of the plot is
elected to the Board of Supervisors of Arlington County. He
convinces the other members of the Board to rewrite the local
zoning ordinances. He becomes a respected figure in the community and is urged to run for the state legislature. But he de-
clines, stating that there is plenty of work to do in one's home
town.

Along these lines, there is another excellent film with a plot
that has to do with political and military things. It's called
The Night of the Field Marshals. The story is simple. Five
five-star generals receive identical letters from the President
telling them that they have been promoted to the rank of field
marshal. The generals are delighted, because not even Eisenhower or MacArthur ever attained to the rank of field mar-

shal. Two days later, the generals receive another letter from the President. The President explains that there has been a terrible error, that the rank of field marshal does not exist in the armed forces of the United States, and that the generals will have to remain generals after all. The five generals accept their demotion with good grace, saying that anyone can make an honest mistake.

For those who like movies about people and animals, I heartily recommend *The Black Camel*. I have to say, however, that the plot is a little complicated. This is a drawback because very young children may find it hard to understand. But here's a summary of what happens. The United States Army is organizing an expeditionary force to invade an oil-rich country in the Middle East. Because the invasion is to be carried out in the dead of night, the Army wishes to use nothing but black camels in the cavalry unit. But there is only one black camel that anyone knows of—the one who lives at the National Zoo. In fact, this is the only jet-black camel in captivity. The Army asks the director of the zoo whether more black camels can be bred. The director says that at least one other black camel, a female, will be necessary if breeding is to be undertaken. Fortunately, another black camel is found, and the two camels produce a camel calf, also jet black. It is this particular black camel after which the movie is named.

The black camel is taken from its parents and raised on an Army base in Arizona. It wins several awards for heroism and comes in first in the camel race. Then the government decides to pursue a policy of reconciliation with the oil-rich kingdom, so the expeditionary force is disbanded. The black camel is reunited with its parents at the National Zoo, and becomes a particular favorite of youngsters who visit the place. This is a heartwarming story, sure to be a favorite with children of all ages!

Of course, the grownups are entitled to something for themselves, and they'll find it if they go to see *All the President's Women*. This film is done in the modern style of *cinéma verité*, and there's no way to tell whether it is a real movie or just a documentary. In fact, it is so realistic that it describes twenty-four hours in the life of the White House typing pool and takes exactly twenty-four hours to run! But don't worry, because there is a nine-hour intermission which leaves plenty of time not only for a full night's sleep but also for a shower and breakfast. In this movie, the plot is also simple but very exciting nonetheless. The White House typing pool of six typists has no more than twenty-four hours to type the final version of the President's State of the Union address. They divide the work into six parts and, by working together, the job is done in only three hours. Because they are so efficient, they have twenty-one hours to do whatever they please. The President is so pleased to learn that his speech will be ready on time that he gives them the rest of the day off. All of them go home and watch the State of the Union address on television.

All of these movies provide a good evening's entertainment. They give real value for the money you spend, and none of them has subtitles. That's why I was able to write about them. I happen to be a slow reader and I miss a lot when I have to follow subtitles. I like American movies because, if you feel like reading, there's certainly no shortage of books and magazines.

The Academy

There is not one great university in the Nation's Capital, not one institution fit to join the Ivy League or the Big Ten. This, as we know, is the result of a plot among the provincials to maintain their sense of superiority over the governing class in the capital. For if there arose in the District of Columbia a collegiate football power the likes of Nebraska or Oklahoma, or a collegiate academic power the likes of Reed or Grinnell, how then could ridicule be heaped upon the uninspired and unlettered bureaucrats who are scorned by even the most untutored member of Congress?

This had been understood from the beginning. The District Elders had known it and had attempted to establish a major center of learning in the District. They had heard years ago that Elihu Yale, who had already developed an intense dislike for John Harvard (he had taken to calling Harvard an "insufferable ass" in his weekly Sunday homilies), was now bent on starting a university of his own. "I'm going to run Jack Harvard out of New England," Elihu had thundered. "When I'm done with him, all anyone will remember is that he used to be in the bed-frame business! That arrogant twit!"

Mr. Harvard professed unconcern. Elihu was notorious for these fits of rage, followed by equally intense fits of depression. He would mope around the house for days on end, mumbling about free will, determinism, and Connecticut politics. "Elihu Yale," Jack Harvard would chuckle, "all anyone will remember about him is that he used to be in the lock business."

The District Elders, even though they knew that Elihu was not the easiest man in the world to deal with, decided to persuade him that his new university belonged in the District of Columbia. When they called on him in New Haven they found him slightly the worse for a visit to Maury's, for he was not above an occasional tankard of ale. "Elihu," they said, "we have a package of tax incentives, a flexible labor supply, and an atmosphere that is more than congenial to the pursuit of knowledge. So why not open up your university in Washington?"

"I prefer New Haven, Connecticut," answered Elihu with a quiet belch.

"New Haven?" they had responded in stunned disbelief. "What is New Haven? Nothing but the terminus of a bankrupt railroad and a graveyard for boring theatricals and tone-deaf musicales! You will bomb in New Haven."

"My wife loves it," mumbled Elihu. "She refuses to leave. All her friends are here, and she thinks that a move to Washington would prove unsettling to our fourteen children. The only place she'll even think about is California, northern California. I have a terrific offer from Leland Stanford to establish a Yale of the West Coast, so why should I move to your malarial swamp? Besides, Leland seems to be a pious man in every respect, so unless you can top his offer, you might as well stop talking. And believe me, I'm not going to bomb in New Haven! I'm not about to let that pompous blivet Jack Harvard run me out of New England!"

The District Elders concluded that they could transact no further business with a man they regarded as a near-psychotic fundamentalist. The negotiations came to an end and they withdrew, amidst Elihu's muttering about pox, predestination, pederasty, and Cambridge, Massachusetts.

For a while, it was believed by the District Elders that nothing useful could come from further contacts with intellectuals and academics, for like the happy families of Tolstoy's *Anna Karenina*, they were all weird in the same way. But they took their civic responsibilities seriously, and when they got wind of the fact that Ezra Cornell was interested in founding a university, they went to call on him in the obscure village of Ithaca, New York. Making their way through a near-blinding snowstorm, and with two of their number already suffering from serious cases of frostbite, they made their slide-show presentation to Mr. Cornell.

"Whatever could appeal to you about this piece of Arctic tundra as a site for a university?" they had wondered aloud. "Better to come to Washington where we can offer you a congenial atmosphere and favorable tax treatment."

But Ezra, already in his dotage, rambled on senescently about the appeal of the countryside, and allowed as that he had already commissioned a university song. Even before the university was opened, it was already the most popular alma mater tune in America.

"It's impossible, just impossible," Ezra had prattled. "People are already coming to Cayuga's waters, and can you imagine their disappointment when they discover there's nothing there, absolutely nothing there, save for a few fur trappers? No, it's quite out of the question to consider locating anywhere else."

And so it went. The District Elders called on John D. Rockefeller, in an attempt to have Rockefeller University built in Washington rather than in Manhattan. Mr. Rockefeller said that it was fine with him, except that he wanted the Elders to know that he planned to open a university of a wholly new sort—one without students. This was obviously unacceptable.

It was all very humiliating. Cornelius Vanderbilt preferred

to open up in Nashville, Tennessee, R. E. B. Baylor preferred Waco. William Marsh Rice preferred Houston. King William and his wife Mary could not be persuaded to move from Richmond, Virginia. Bishop Berkeley wanted his place within easy commuting distance of San Francisco. E. H. Harriman was too stingy to found a university—or even a foundation—and J. P. Morgan was interested only in founding libraries.

It is only with the greatest reluctance that the Elders came to abandon their hope of having a university founded and endowed by one of the great captains of industry, one of the legendary robber barons. "It's too late for that now," one of them sighed. "We must now seek to tap the newer fortunes, and appeal to the new first families of America." And so they were off again. They would soon be calling on Colonel Sanders.

Patrons, Scholars, and Humanists

It is only in recent years that the nation has become interested in the advancement of the arts and sciences in the Capital. The traditional sponsors of these activities now take it as their civic responsibility to raise Washington's level of achievement in these realms to at least the heights attained in the other great capitals in the history of the world. America's great philanthropic institutions have been pioneers in this important effort, as even a cursory glance at their recent grants will indicate.

The Bollingen Foundation will support the composition of an epic poem, at least 14,000 lines in length, chronicling the history of the Bureau of Reclamation. The poet will receive $42,000, which will allow him to devote two years to the poem's creation. It will describe the wanderings of a great dam builder who, downed in an air crash in the Rocky Mountains, builds dams throughout the West during the thirty-year period it takes him to return to his faithful wife in Chicago.

The John Simon Guggenheim Foundation has announced that it will commission a large mural, sixty feet by twenty, wherein the artist will record the achievements of the previous administration. The mural will be painted on the ceiling of Washington's best-known Reform Jewish congregation.

The medical science division of the Rockefeller Foundation has made a grant to two physiologists in the Capital who will study the effects of encephalitis on attendance at congressional hearings. If the research establishes the proper correlation, the Foundation is prepared to subsidize a large-scale spraying program to rid the Capital of tzetze flies.

The National Bureau of Economic Research has agreed to fund the studies of two economists who wish to test their new theory that there is a correlation between rising prices on the one hand and inflation on the other. The economists will also receive a matching grant from the Department of Commerce.

The American Historical Association has awarded its annual research fellowship to a young historian from Wyoming who wishes to investigate what became of those individuals who received the Nobel Peace Prize during the 1950's. Part of the grant will finance field research to see whether anyone remembers their names, so that the historian can be told who they were.

The American Political Science Association has commissioned two political sociologists to investigate why it is that the American voter tends to vote for one or the other candidates that appear on the ballot. This is part of a larger project in comparative politics which seeks to establish an explanation for the failure of Eurocommunism to appear in North America.

The Mobil Oil Corporation Educational Foundation will back another piece of survey research, a sampling of elite opinion, to determine whether consumers really don't like paying higher prices for gasoline, or whether they are merely *saying* that they don't like to.

The National Education Association, determined to upgrade the teaching of civics in the public schools, has commissioned a new syllabus. The syllabus will explain once and for all why the constitutional monarchy we now have is an improvement over the proportional-representation parliamentary system we used to have prior to the Civil War.

Five anonymous donors have contributed funds to commission America's leading sculptor to cast, in bronze, a full-scale replica of a McDonnell Douglas DC-10, to be installed on the grounds of the National Air and Space Museum.

The Society for the Preservation of Native American Folk Art has made a grant to Mrs. Pierre Defarge of Baton Rouge, Louisiana. Mrs. Defarge will knit the entire history of the United States in a series of ten queen-sized blankets. Replicas of the blankets will then be marketed in order to raise funds for support of our team in the next Olympics.

The Asia Society has commissioned a translation of the *Federalist Papers* into modern Bengali, to be given to the President of Bangladesh during his next state visit to the United States.

The American Society of Actuaries has commissioned three actuaries in Washington to discover why it is that beneficiaries of life insurance policies do not very often turn back the money they receive after the death of a loved one.

The Institute for Advanced Study at Princeton University has given funds to a physicist at a local university so that he may test his hypothesis that the fifty-five-mile-per-hour speed limit is inconsistent with Einstein's theory of relativity.

The trustees of the Henry Clay Frick Collection in New York City have made a large cash grant to five Washington art dealers. The dealers will now be able to snap up everything in sight at wildly inflated prices, in order to provide local artists with an incentive to paint more pictures.

A large foundation in the Midwest, choosing to remain anonymous, has offered a substantial cash grant to any young and aspiring Washington novelist who can guess the foundation's name. The same foundation has also offered to endow a Nobel War Prize, to be given to the individual or individuals responsible for instigating the most destructive war during the preceding year.

The Center for the Study of Democratic Institutions has established a $10,000 prize, to be awarded annually for the best essay on the topic "The Relevance of Oriental Despotism in the Modern World."

A rich businessman has endowed a Peter Lorre Chair of Pyrotechnics at a local university, so that foreign students can be better instructed in the practical political benefits of high explosives. He has also established a prize of $25,000 for the first foreign student who succeeds in making an atomic bomb.

The Oberlin Conservatory of Music has commissioned a Washington composer who will write a three-hour oratorio, based on variations of the basic musical line of "God Bless America." The oratorio will be premiered next spring, one night after the first performance by the Washington Opera Society of a new opera. The opera has already been commissioned by the Korea-America Friendship Society; it is based on the life of the late President Park Chung Hee.

The Washington Ballet Theatre has received a large grant which will allow it to revive its classic production of *Appealia,* the first ballet ever based on a case argued before the Supreme Court. Funds for the production have been made available by the American Bar Association and the Association of Trial Lawyers. When the ballet was first staged five years ago, it was the subject of enormous controversy; the National Organization of Women protested when the female lawyers wore tutus as they danced before the nine dirty old Justices.

Finally, a group of local restaurant owners has, at long last, commissioned a new fight song for the Washington Redskins. Entitled "Song for Team, Cheerleaders, and Season Ticket Holders," the song is only eighteen seconds long, and because the composer is a devoted disciple of twelve-tone music, the song has no discernible melody. But since the new fight song was introduced, the Redskins have not lost a home game. The tune frightens the wits out of the visiting team.

Literary Persuasion

For several years, the editor of the *Washington Review of Books* had attempted to arrange a meeting between Senator Larethan Jerome Wimbol—who, at age one hundred and forty-six, was the oldest man ever to serve in the Senate—and the Latin-American novelist Gabriel García Márquez, who had once written of a mythical village in South America, the inhabitants of which had attained to vast and great ages. The editor had thought that this would be amusing. Wimbol had resisted the effort. He seldom read fiction and, when he did, he preferred that it be written in English. Besides, he had heard that Márquez was a man of "progressive politics," not likely to get on with a man like Wimbol, who, at twenty quadrennial conventions of his party, had always been called "a great American."

Yet Márquez was intrigued by the prospect. The ancient persons who peopled his masterwork, *One Hundred Years of*

Solitude, were all products of his own vivid imagination. It had never occurred to him that there could exist a man like Wimbol. And yet, if a man could attain to nearly one hundred and fifty years and show few if any signs of senility, he might be worth immortalizing in a monumental work of art.

The meeting was finally arranged in the offices of the *Washington Review.* Wimbol was, as was his habit, punctual. Márquez, being a Latin American, was thirty minutes late. "Who is this Márquez?" Wimbol had asked of his staff the morning of the appointment. His staff had patiently explained that he was a great novelist who wrote about old people. "Ah," Wimbol had said, "one of those 'gray power' types. Got it." The staff moaned. "No," they explained, "Márquez is the author of international best sellers." And they had handed Wimbol a black briefing book, filled with information to prime him for the interview.

"Good afternoon, Senator," said Márquez cheerfully, "I am Gabriel García Márquez, author of *One Hundred Years of Solitude.*"

"What's so great about that?" said Wimbol. "My staff tells me you plagiarized the title from the autobiography of one of the captains of American industry, the hi-fi tycoon Avery Fisher."

"Who is he?" said Márquez.

"The author of *One Hundred Watts of Amplitude,*" said Wimbol, looking up from his black briefing book.

"*Caramba,*" said Márquez.

"Here's another one," said Wimbol. "A first-person account by one of our astronauts, Frank Borman—*One Hundred Miles of Altitude.*"

"I, the great Márquez, accused of plagiarism, by a gringo!" exclaimed Márquez. "Truly unbelievable."

"Here's another one," said Wimbol, glancing down at his briefing book. "Yes, a book by the great mariner Sir Francis Chichester, called *One Hundred Leagues of Latitude.*"

"Lies, all lies," said Márquez. "Gringos cashing in on my genius."

"The Holy Father, Pope John Paul II, is surely no gringo, and he has written a book called *One Hundred Lines of Beatitude*," answered Wimbol testily.

"You idiot," said Márquez, "can you not understand that these are people who have plagiarized from me, not me from them?"

"It's more than a coincidence," answered Wimbol, shaking his head. "Last year when I threw four boring constituents out of my office, one of them sent me a book by Emily Post called *One Hundred Forms of Gratitude*. And when I am in need of spiritual replenishment, I turn to Norman Vincent Peale's inspirational work, *One Hundred Routes to Platitude*. I am quite sure, sir, that the eminent Reverend Dr. Peale has never heard of you."

"Nor I of him," answered Márquez icily.

"You deny the influence of cross-cultural contact in the formation of contemporary literature?" asked Wimbol.

"I deny no such thing," said Márquez. "I am an intellectual."

"And yet you tell me," continued Wimbol, "that you have never encountered the seminal work of our great spokesman for the oppressed, the Reverend Jesse Jackson, author of *One Hundred Hues of Negritude?* I find that hard to believe."

"I have great sympathy with the aspirations of the oppressed minorities in the United States," said Márquez solemnly, "and I will certainly get a copy of the Reverend Jackson's book and read it."

"Good," said Wimbol, "and while you're at it, I commend to you the masterwork by the eminent theological dogmatist, the Swiss thinker Karl Barth, *One Hundred Rules of Certitude*. It is a useful antidote to the dangerous notions being bandied about in Latin America by left-wing bishops." And having said this, Wimbol smiled inwardly, for he was pleased that he had been so well briefed. His staff never failed him.

Márquez himself also paused to ponder. Here, before his very eyes, was the real surreal. A living, breathing, one-hundred-forty-six-year-old man who rattled off bizarre book titles. Could anything be more suggestive to a man of creative bent?

The editor, who had remained silent all the while, interjected himself into the conversation for the first time. "Come to think of it, Gabriel," he said, "I remember now that we once reviewed a biography by an eminent musicologist called *One Life of Dietrich Buxtahude.*"

Wimbol glanced down at his briefing book, but could not find the title. He did find *One Hundred Hymns by Buxtahude,* and he assumed that this must be the work under discussion.

"You know," said Wimbol, "whenever I speak to a large gathering, I find it useful to begin with a joke or two. My favorite anthology of American humor is edited by Don Rickles. It's called *One Hundred Jokes, Allverycrude.*"

"Who publishes that?" asked the editor. "I'd like to get a copy."

"I have several, and I will send you one," said Wimbol.

Coffee was then served. Márquez thought to himself that perhaps the Americans were attempting to break down his customary notions of space and time so as to create wholly new effects. But he wasn't at all sure.

The editor spoke again. "A friend in New York just sent me a fascinating cookbook by Julia Child. It's called *One Hundred Ways to Cookfrenchfood,* and nothing in it is fattening."

But Wimbol was scarcely paying attention. He continued to flip the pages of his briefing book and he noticed under the heading "music," where the reference to the hymns of Buxtahude appeared, there was another title. He raised his eyes once again. "Mr. Márquez," he said, "I should acquaint you with a classic work, vital to the understanding of the history of American popular music. It's by the late, great Glenn Miller, and it's entitled *One Hundred Notes of Inthemood.*"

"I've read that," said the editor, "and it certainly does capture the spirit of youthful exuberance and national unity which characterized the generation of the early forties!"

"I haven't read that," acknowledged Márquez, "but in order to gain a better understanding of the just struggle being

waged by OPEC against the imperialists, I did read the autobiography of the late King Ibn Saud of Saudi Arabia called *One
Hundred Children Inmybrood.*"

"That's the spirit!" exclaimed the Senator and the editor simultaneously. "Now you're getting it! You can do it, Gabriel,
if you really try!"

"Do you really think so?" asked Márquez demurely.

"I think he's got it!" said the editor, slapping his knee.
"There'll be no stopping him now!"

"Yes," said Márquez, "I can feel it coming on. I remember
now. It's the autobiography of Edith Piaf, *One Hundred Love
Songs Thati'vecooed.*"

"Excellent, Gabriel," said the two others approvingly.

"And what about the autobiography of Thom McAn, *One
Hundred Million Feeti'veshoed?*" said Gabriel enthusiastically.

"Close, very close, Gabriel," said the editor, "but it should
be 'shod' not 'shoed.'"

"Ah," said Gabriel, "the past participles of your language
can make someone plumb *loco* in the *cabeza.*"

"We must continue this at dinner!" said the editor, rubbing
his hands together. "There's no telling what we can accom-
plish if we go on for a few more hours."

"I must return to my work," said Wimbol, "but do go on
without me. Meanwhile, Gabriel, I find you a not altogether
unacceptable sort, and I would like to give you a signed copy
of one of my favorite books. Something for the coffee table, a
collection of beautiful color prints, compiled and edited by
Hugh Hefner, *One Hundred Poses Inthenude.*"

"*Gracias, Senador,*" said Márquez. "And I shall immortalize
you. You are what is known in my own native country as a
dirty old man, the only kind of old man truly worth writing
about."

Book III

BRINGING OUT THE BAGGAGE

A Little Bit of Soul

We decided to drive out to Dorley's for a couple of drinks, a light supper, and some of the music. Dorley's was definitely becoming the place to go. In fact, Dorley's had been written up as the leader in bringing back the quiet jazz sound, the sound we had all heard in the background of the old movies on the TV late show.

Dorley's did not disappoint us. The jazz group was outstanding. The more I listened, the more I realized that it was the piano player who made the difference. His music had a clean sound, assertive but not overstated. His interpretations of some of the old standards, though clearly original, still struck one as definitive. What's more, he looked very familiar.

Suddenly I realized that it was Spiro Agnew.

I picked up my drink and walked over to the piano. It was Spiro Agnew, without any doubt. He was backed up by a bass, drums, and a very mellow electric guitar. Sitting on his piano was a large brandy snifter stuffed with five- and ten-dollar bills, obviously gratuities deposited by big spenders with special requests.

Spiro looked up and, without missing a note, invited me to sit down next to him. I had always been amazed by the ability of pianists in night spots to converse and play at the same time, even though I had seen it dozens of times on the late show. As I sat next to him on the piano bench, I was impressed once again with his effortless facility at the keyboard.

"Spiro," I said, "what have you been up to?"

"Oh," Spiro responded, "my group and I got tired of one-nighters, so we decided to play here on a regular basis." He shifted, effortlessly as usual, from "Deep Purple" to "I Can't Get Started with You."

"You know," he continued, "I guess I first realized I could make a go of this back in '72. Nixon invited me to sit down and play something for the Shah during one of those White House dinners. Everyone there recognized that I played much better than Nixon. That really got Nixon furious, especially after the Shah said that nobody played my style of funky piano in Teheran. Do you know that the Shah invited me to play at his great blowout in Persepolis? That really drove Nixon up the wall, because he wasn't asked. I think all my problems with him started that night." And, without missing a note, he left "I Can't Get Started with You" and moved right into "I Wish You Love."

I was impressed, because not even Georges Feyer or Peter Duchin could negotiate the transition between those two tunes with such grace.

The guitarist took a few bars as Spiro took two sips from a glass of ginger ale supplied by a waiter. Then Spiro sang the lead-in. And with that, he motioned to the crowd to join in; they responded with the first verse.

The crowd continued to sing on its own, and Spiro said to me, "That's a terrific lyric!" He punctuated the lyric with a run of sevenths that was marvelously appropriate. Then Spiro took the solo. He gestured to the crowd to join in.

The applause had not yet died down, but Spiro had already shifted from "I Wish You Love" to "Candy Man." "It's all a matter of knowing the basic chord structures," said Spiro. "Once you've got them down, you can play practically anything."

We were joined at the piano by a lanky fellow who spoke with a pronounced Oklahoma accent. "Spiro, old buddy," he drawled, "we met a few years back at the annual dinner of the American Petroleum Institute."

"Right," Spiro nodded.

"My wife and I were wonderin' if you would play something to remind us of the old days," continued the Oklahoman. "What about 'Danny Boy'?" He slipped a twenty in Spiro's brandy snifter.

"You bet," winked Spiro, and he eased into "Danny Boy," giving it country and western overtones that brought a smile to the face of the Oklahoman.

"Their eyes always light up when I play the old tunes," said Spiro. The waiter brought another glass of ginger ale and, by now, Spiro was into the first few bars of "I Left My Heart in San Francisco."

"Spiro," I said, "you play with great expressiveness. You really feel the music."

"Well," said Spiro, "the fact is that I've suffered. I've been through it. Even the black musicians admire the way I play the blues." And with that, he went into "Sometimes I Feel Like a Motherless Child." As soon as he had finished that great standard, he sang again, this time in a voice that convinced all of us that Louis Armstrong himself was in the room. It was that great favorite, "Nobody Knows You When You're Down and Out." The crowd applauded.

"I really used to break them up when I'd do 'I've Got a Right to Sing the Blues,'" Spiro remarked, "but we don't play that tune any more. One of my old friends, Chuck Colson, told me it smacks of self-pity."

Then and there, I realized that Spiro had paid his dues.

My mind must have been wandering, because, when I next heard the music, Spiro was already in the middle of "Bridge over Troubled Water." As his hands moved gracefully over the keys, Spiro reminisced. "In the old days," he said, "I never related to the contemporary tunes. I guess it was Nixon's influence. He and Pat would get down in the dumps and they would ask me to play some Harold Arlen. Their favorite tune of his was 'Come Rain or Come Shine.' It used to perk up their spirits. Sometimes Bob, and all those guys named John, the lawyers, the accountants, Manolo—everybody—would join in on the last line.

I had to agree. Spiro's playing had a touch of genuine elegance; it was far more sophisticated than his old East Room style.

I complimented Spiro on his playing and told him I'd been away from my table too long and had to return to my guests. Without missing a note, he managed to shake my hand and remind me that his group had cut an album for Capitol Records. I made a mental note to pick up a copy because I wanted to reproduce the warm atmosphere of Dorley's in my own living room.

"Remarkable," I said to my guests when I rejoined them, "the man's a real individual."

We stayed for Spiro's next set, and we would have stayed even later, but it was almost 2 A.M. I asked for the bill. I usually pay cash, but this time I tossed my American Express card to the waiter because I wanted the receipt as a memento of that extraordinary evening. As I tipped the waiter, I remembered that I had forgotten Spiro's brandy snifter. I returned to the piano and, not to be outdone by an Oklahoman, I dropped in a twenty of my own.

"Take care, pal," said Spiro.

By the time we reached the door, Spiro and the group were well into "To the Good Life."

Houses of Worship

Much like the great European capitals which it strives to emulate, the city of Washington is known for its beautiful churches. Varied in architecture, wide-ranging in affiliation, these structures have come to symbolize the religious foundations of the Republic and the moral basis of our political life.

Best known, of course, is the Church of Our Lady of the Legislature, only two blocks from the lesser-known though architecturally more interesting parish of St. Samuel the Lawgiver. As every Sunday-school student knows, there have been but two authenticated sightings of the Virgin in this hemisphere, and the Church of Our Lady of the Legislature marks one. The story is often repeated by the tour guides. Karen Aims, a legislative secretary, was on her way to her apartment, pondering the ultimatum given to her earlier that day by the congressman for whom she worked. Submit, he had said, or forfeit all hope of advancement in this office. She had said she

would think it over. Surely, it was a critical decision in the life
of a twenty-year-old young woman, and a test of the faith
which had been instilled in her by her devout and altogether
God-fearing parents.

It was dusk, and Karen was seated on an ordinary bench in
a small park in the vicinity of the Capitol, when the Virgin
appeared to her. At first she could hardly believe her eyes, but
the visage was clear and precise. For at least thirty seconds,
she saw the Virgin with an animated expression on her face,
wagging her finger in no uncertain terms. Karen had rubbed
her eyes, fearing delirium, but upon reopening her eyes, the
figure was still present, its finger still wagging. Yet this was an
event that required corroboration. Karen fell to her knees, and
implored Mary to remain but five minutes longer. And then
she rose and sprinted to the closest Capitol Hill bar, where
she gathered together three friends and, with them, ran back
to the site. "There is moral support for us out there," Karen
said to her disbelieving co-workers. The four returned to the
park; each confirmed what the others saw plainly before them,
the Virgin herself, her finger still wagging.

The word of four witnesses could not be denied and, after
some years, the sighting was authenticated by the proper religious authorities. They decreed the construction of a church
on the site, zoning variances were obtained, and the funds for
construction were easily raised around the country. Today, the
Church of Our Lady of the Legislature is a haven for all of
those, of whatever preference, who seek to escape from sexual
harassment and who strive for the inner strength to combat it.

Across from the Treasury Department, of course, is the
lovely Shrine of St. Accountus the Counselor, sometimes
called, familiarly, St. Accountus of the Loophole. St. Accountus, as the Shrine's literature explains, was a novice in a
small monastery in Rheims, assigned to keeping the books and
to preparing the tax returns of the abbot. He is revered in his
profession, for he was the first man to discover a loophole in
the famous seventeenth-century French tax regulations that
had been promulgated by the Sun King, Louis XIV. Ac-

countus went on to discover still others in that sloppily worded code. Each year, the richest French nobles would make substantial contributions to the monastery, and the abbot, in turn, would allow Accountus to prepare their tax returns as well as his own. By the late 1690's, as the Shrine's pamphlet goes on to point out, at least two thirds of the income of the French nobility was sheltered, an extraordinary percentage in those days, far in excess of what had been achieved in neighboring Belgium. Accountus' beatification, and then his canonization in 1771, were both something of an afterthought. Long before the formal steps were taken, he had already come to be thought of as the patron saint of his profession. And yet, so far as Church historians know, the Shrine of St. Accountus the Counselor is the only church in the world which bears his name. By great good fortune, the feast day of St. Accountus is May 13, the day before the annual examination given by the local government to those who seek to become certified public accountants. It is now traditional that candidates for the examination gather at the Shrine on that day to pray for success. Most remarkable is the fact that since candidates began pledging the first 15 percent of their income to the Shrine should they pass the test, the success rate on the CPA examination has soared to well over 85 percent. This is more than double the success rate for the years before this practice began. In truth, the Shrine has become rich indeed. It is the only church in Washington which uses handheld calculators (with both plain-language and digital readouts) in place of the customary missal.

It has been said by many visitors who have taken the tour of Washington churches conducted daily by the Fellowship of Christian Bureaucrats that the most moving moments come at the end—at the Cathedral of St. Hilda of the Canapé. It is true that it is an imposing structure, the second-tallest building in the city, easily visible from aircraft approaching the local airport. As the tour guides explain, the Cathedral has come to symbolize a central feature of Washington life. The Hilda in question was, of course, Hilda Olginsen, the pro-

prietress of Washington's most distinguished and reliable ca-
tering firm. She had survived and prospered, despite the
changing food fads across the decades. Once called upon to
prepare simple snacks on plain white bread, she shifted effortlessly through the philo-Semitic era which required the serving of smoked fish and bagels at Sunday brunches, and then
adjusted easily to the Islamic revival period, when recipes for
chomos were as closely guarded as the nation's military secrets.

The Cathedral itself sits on the site of what was once the
Scrivener estate. Mrs. Scrivener—actually Hubert Scrivener's
second wife—was the most fashionable and powerful hostess
of her era. Though her parties were grand and lavish and exceptionally well attended, the truth is that Sonia Scrivener
was a compulsive worrier. It was necessary that all her parties
"go right," and before especially significant events, she was
even given to praying for their success. So concerned was she
by one gathering which she had planned that she made a vow
to God. "If you will deliver to me this one last triumph before
my impending death, I will consecrate the ground upon which
my great tent sits, the tent in which I will gather for luncheon
this coming Sunday the greatest collection of guests I have
ever assembled, and build upon it a house of worship the like
of which has not yet been seen in this city," she had said to
the Lord.

As all present that day will attest, the event was indeed a
triumph. It was front-page news. Such was Mrs. Scrivener's
power that it was a command performance. The former Shah
of Iran and the Ayatollah Khomeini both accepted their invitations and it was during lunch that their historic reconciliation was achieved. Long after the other guests had departed, the retired monarch and the unusually effervescent
Ayatollah were seen strolling through the Scrivener gardens,
engaged in friendly and animated conversation.

Mrs. Scrivener, though an octogenarian in decline, could
not contain her delight. "Aren't they marvelous!" she had said
to one of the reporters present. "I mean, the Shah is *so* regal,

and the Ayatollah, well, I mean he's a dear. He's so—what shall I say?—so *Islamic!*" In her characteristic fashion, she attributed it all to Hilda's hors d'oeuvres.

As good as her word, the great dowager struck the tent on her lawn, and went so far as to order the demolition of the fixed structures on the property. She contributed a substantial sum for the house of worship she had vowed to build—some speculate as much as $32 million, although the exact sum has never been revealed. It was decided to name the Cathedral after Hilda Olginsen, who had collapsed in a swoon and later expired, after the Ayatollah had complimented her on the canapés by patting her on the cheek and saying, "Yummy. The caviar is even better than what we have at home!"

It was inevitable that other Washington hostesses would begin to pray to Hilda's departed soul. Such prayers produced miracles in such large number that no one was able to doubt either their authority or their appearance as a result of Hilda's intercessions. She was soon canonized.

On Saturday afternoons, there is no busier place than the Cathedral of St. Hilda of the Canapé. Hundreds of hostesses mill about in the nave, dozens more fill the apse, candles are lit and prayers are offered. And the supplicants come from every walk of life, from the rich and powerful whose tables will, on Saturday evening, glitter with sterling and crystal, to the young and aspiring whose tables will be graced only by plain china procured in the discount housewares stores.

For as it was said by Mrs. Scrivener on her deathbed, "the grand dinner party requires more than the presence of beautiful glassware and gleaming plates and scintillating guests. God must also be present."

Bedclothes

The Ku Klux Klan had met with some success in reviving itself as a national political force, but the Klan revival of the late 1970's had never really gotten off the ground. The Klan's crusade for the repeal of the Thirteenth Amendment had gotten nowhere, lost as it was in the larger shuffle of proposed constitutional amendments having to do with women, taxes, and buses. It was therefore inevitable that the Klan would seek the services of a Washington representative in order to magnify its impact on the political process.

This was not easy. The Klan lacks cachet, and is not the sort of client that a political consultant will readily take on. But ever since the landmark Supreme Court ruling that the right to engage a political consultant is implied by the guarantees of the First Amendment, a good bit of money has been made in representing otherwise noxious causes. Indeed, there are firms which specialize in nothing else. One in particular—

Klasse and Deklasse, Inc.—has become the place to go if one chooses to remain outside the bounds of polite political discourse.

Thus, the bargain was struck between the Klan's Deputy Grand Dragon for Imagery and Andrew Deklasse himself, one of the founders of the firm.

"You'll feel right at home with us," Deklasse had assured the Dragon. "We are very experienced with people with your particular problem. We represent the timber cutters, the whale killers, the DDT sprayers, and the Ad Hoc Coalition to Taunt the Handicapped. You may remember the work we did for the importers of liquefied natural gas when their tanker blew up in Baltimore harbor. We turned that thirty-seven-day fire into a major tourist attraction, so that the public, far from fearing such explosions, came to demand more of them. And we convinced one petroleum company to come out with Petroskiff, the toy that has replaced the skateboard; now millions of Americans have discovered the joys of skimming across oil slicks, propelled by the breezes at previously unattainable rates of speed! Should I go on?"

"Nope," said the Dragon. "You fellows sound like what we need. Whatever your fee, it will be more than worth it. Where do we begin?"

"This is the toughest case we've ever had," said Deklasse. "I hardly know where to begin. You may have the most discredited organization in America. But there's nothing we like better than a real challenge! The transformation of the Ku Klux Klan is going to be the greatest triumph in the history of Washington political consulting!" exclaimed Deklasse, rubbing his hands together in eager anticipation.

Deklasse buzzed for his briefing team, and in a few minutes they were in his office with large charts, an easel, and a slide projector and screen. They wheeled in a videotape machine and a television set to which they attached it. Two attractive young women brought in a tea cart containing a coffee urn and a plate piled high with small sandwiches. Deklasse ordered the shades drawn and the lights turned out.

"Let me show what we've worked up," said Deklasse.

"Good deal," said the Dragon.

The first slide was a blown-up picture of the Imperial Wizard leading his minions down a southern highway.

"Let's start at the top," said Deklasse, and his assistant laid the pointer on the Wizard's conical headdress.

"Now this is altogether wrong," said Deklasse. "The shape of it is too ambiguous, too pointed, too threatening, too reminiscent of a dunce cap. It is neither introspective nor even reflective. May I have the first overlay please?"

One of the assistants placed the overlay in the projector, so that a new headdress appeared almost magically in place of the old on the screen. The new headdress resembled an over-size beret. It was of pale beige, and had a bit of nub to it, probably made out of corduroy or soft chamois. It sat lightly and easily on the head of the Wizard.

"Now the mask, please," said Deklasse, and the assistant laid the pointer on the piece of cloth with two eyeholes that covered the face of the Wizard. "Because," continued Deklasse, "the eyeholes constrict the field of the vision of the wearer, the mask conveys a certain narrowness in the *mind* of the wearer. That is easily remedied, however. May I have the second overlay please?"

The assistant repeated the procedure, and there appeared on the screen a new facial covering. It was a piece of pale green plastic, a replica of the sort attached to the helmets of motorcyclists. "Yes," said Deklasse, "it preserves anonymity, yet it suggests openness, even friendliness. And it has the practical benefit of shielding the eyes from the glare of the sun."

"That sure is an improvement," said the Dragon, "and I could kick myself for not having thought of it!"

"Well," said Deklasse, "that's what we're here for—to think of things that people would not think of themselves. Now, let's move on to the robe itself." The assistant laid his pointer on the Wizard's robe, and then moved the pointer up and down and sideways to emphasize the point that was to come.

"We have to tell you," continued Deklasse, "that the robe is an absolute disaster and needs to be completely redesigned."

"Not the robe too?" moaned the Dragon.

"I'm afraid so," said Deklasse.

"What's wrong with it?" asked the Dragon.

"*Everything*," answered Deklasse. "In the first place, it is totally anachronistic. There is not a single American under the age of twenty who has ever seen a white bedsheet. If you don't think so, just try to buy a plain white muslin bedsheet at any department store! They won't have the vaguest idea of what you're talking about. Earth tones, my friend, earth tones —or at least pastels. That's what a sheet is these days and you will have to get used to it. May I have the next overlay please?"

In an instant, the Wizard's plain white sheet had been replaced by a blinding flash of swirls, stripes, and patterns, and across the chest of the Wizard was an unmistakable logo, the bold signature of VERA.

"Vera," asked the Dragon, "who's Vera?"

"A prominent sheet maker," answered Deklasse. "You will just have to accept the fact that the salvation of the Ku Klux Klan lies in designer sheets."

"What's her last name?" asked the Dragon.

"Nobody knows," answered Deklasse somberly. "Some speculate that she was a love child and that she doesn't even have a last name."

"I don't think we will be able to go for that," said the Dragon. "After all, if we stand for anything, it's for male supremacy. It's ridiculous for any respectable Klansman to parade in a sheet designed by a woman. I'm afraid this is out of the question."

"Oh," said Deklasse, "there are others to choose from. Let's try another overlay."

The assistant supplied one, and this time the Wizard was wearing a robe that seemed to be nothing but a huge swath of blue denim, exactly the color of blue jeans in fact. Once again, a signature was boldly placed across the Wizard's chest—CALVIN KLEIN.

"Now, that sure is a curious name," said the Dragon as he read off the letters. "Calvin is fine, but the Klein is a bit doubtful. In Alabama, we think of Klein as a Jewish name. If there's one thing we in the Klan stand for, why, it's anti-Semitism! Everybody knows that. How can our Imperial Wizard wear a robe with the name of a Jew on it?"

"I suppose one can wander too far from one's origins in designing a new image," said Deklasse ruefully. "But I think we have a way out of this impasse. Let's try another overlay."

A flick of the slide projector and the Wizard was now wearing what appeared to be a thin-silk robe, almost transparent, the most sensual bedsheet that had yet been displayed. It was pale yellow. And the signature was unmistakable—DIANE VON FURSTENBERG.

The Dragon seemed pleased by this. "I think that von Furstenberg was the name of one of Hitler's most imaginative generals, if I'm not mistaken. So I'm sure our Imperial Wizard wouldn't mind wearing his name on his robe."

The group took a break for sandwiches and coffee, and paused to admire what had been achieved thus far. A rather drab and unimaginatively dressed Imperial Wizard had been transformed into a contemporary figure of immediate aesthetic appeal. The Deputy Grand Dragon had to marvel at it.

"We better take up where we left off," said Deklasse. "There's one more detail we have to attend to before we are able to unveil the Klan of the eighties and proceed to ordering these new outfits for all of your members to parade in. I have to talk to you about your wooden cross."

"Our cross?" inquired the Dragon. "Surely you aren't about to suggest that we give up our wooden cross. Why, it's been our trademark for generations."

"Oh, not at all," answered Deklasse. "Actually, the cross is quite a nice touch. A lot of good work has been done on it already. Our survey data show that people used to respond to it

negatively—symbol of agony and all that. It used to put people off, but, thanks to some of our colleagues in this business,
it now tends to connote love, warmth, caring, feeling, and,
most of all, *concern*. So we've got something to work with.
It's just that the material has to be changed."

"What's wrong with good old-fashioned wood?" asked the
Dragon, appearing somewhat puzzled. "It burns very nicely."

"That's my point precisely!" exclaimed Deklasse. "Good old-
fashioned wood has got to be replaced by good new-fashioned
wood!"

"New-fashioned wood?" said the Dragon, this time appearing more puzzled than ever. "Wood is wood."

"Teak," said Deklasse. "Laminated teak. Solid teak if you
want to lay out the money. If not, teak veneer. But teak it
should be. Well, maybe Philippine mahogany would also do.
No, teak is better."

"What kind of wood is teak?" asked the Dragon.

"Very nice," said Deklasse, "quite nice in fact. It comes
from Thailand in the main, and you can make practically anything out of it—wastebaskets, ice buckets, salad forks, whatever you like. Even crosses. Teak is the universal wood, just
as water is the universal solvent."

"Gee, I don't know about that," said the Dragon, scratching
his chin. "After all, if there's one thing the Ku Klux Klan
stands for, why, it's nativism. I don't know whether we ought
to be making our crosses out of foreign-grown wood."

"Take our word for it," said Deklasse, with a tone of slight
impatience creeping into his voice, "a teak cross is the perfect
thing, a matchless blending of traditional symbol with a modern material. A teak cross, don't you see, whatever its size, can
have a place in every modern home or apartment. A small one
will sit nicely on a teak coffee table, a large one will stand
nicely right next to a large teak planter. The mail-order potential is staggering. But, more important than that, it has wonderful connotations of white supremacy. You see, everything
in Scandinavia is made out of teak, and everybody knows it.
Don't you see? Scandinavian—which means *Nordic*."

"You mean," said the Dragon, "that this teak stuff is white folks' wood?"

"Without doubt," answered Deklasse, his voice now beginning to rise to a feverish pitch. "TEAK IS THE WOOD OF THE ARYAN RACE! It is the wood of ski lodges. Have you ever in your life seen a black person skiing? I tell you, my friend, just the slightest hint that yours is an organization that can keep the slopes lily white, and Northerners will flock to your banner in unprecedented numbers! But it has to be done subtly, of course. That is the genius of the package we have designed for you." A smile of self-satisfaction, even of triumph, began to spread across Deklasse's face.

"Hmmm," said the Dragon. "That is something to think about. If you can't keep them out of the schools, you can at least keep them off the slopes."

"A powerful subliminal message," acknowledged Deklasse. "And it will help out some of our other clients, too, I will have to admit. Distract their attention from nuclear power, and get them thinking about something concrete that really matters to them, rather than worrying about these empty abstractions about what the world will look like in four or five centuries when there are piles of nuclear waste all over the place."

"God damn," said the Dragon, slapping his leg. "You Yankees are pretty clever. I guess that's why you run things."

"I suppose we know what we're doing," acknowledged Deklasse.

The rest of the details were easily managed. And the following winter, the United Klans of America chartered a caravan of buses and headed West. Atop the highest mountain overlooking the settlement of Alta, Utah, they held a giant rally. And with great solemnity, they set afire the largest teak cross that had ever been fashioned in a Scandinavian workshop. As Deklasse had predicted, it was a great media triumph, the first the Klan had known in many years.

The Noble Experiment

It had to happen sooner or later, and it finally did, when the thirty-ninth state ratified the Amendment. Henceforth, there would be a ban on the transport and sale in interstate commerce of what the airlines had come to refer to as "smoking materials." The Emphysema Remission Amendment —ERA in popular parlance—did indeed have a curious origin. It was not originally the creation of old temperance advocates, nor of other remnants of the old Prohibition movement. Rather, it began in a conspiracy among owners of major-league baseball teams who had calculated the expense of sweeping up cigarette butts after each of their home games, and had concluded that the cost of such maintenance cut too deeply into their profit margin. Twenty-seven states had ratified the Amendment before this came to light but, by then, the proponents had enough momentum to bring around the recalcitrant state legislatures.

It was an experiment not without nobility. In that it affected interstate commerce only, it was still perfectly possible to move to one of the tobacco-growing states and smoke contentedly to the limit of one's lungs. And it had brought prosperity to previously blighted areas. Like gambling casinos, smoking resorts attracted a substantial number of tourists to the states where they were established.

Politics surely had something to do with it. The smoke-filled room had always been in bad odor, especially in the Federal City. And much was made of the ceremony which followed upon ratification, when the last smoke-filled room in Washington, D.C., was aired out. The Speaker of the House had been called upon to officiate. He came bearing a bottle of Breath o' Pine, and threw open the windows at just the right moment. The wire service photograph was prominently displayed all across America.

It is, of course, too early to render more than a preliminary judgment on the effects of this new national commitment. It is true that people are, in the main, living longer, but fewer five-act plays are being written. It is possible to see better inside arenas where basketball games are being played, but the clarity of the air has made it easier for the referees to observe the misconduct of the players, and many more fouls are being called. For some reason, the boom in bootleg cigarettes that some had anticipated has failed to materialize. Millions of cigarette machines, some of them smashed to smithereens by more militant supporters of the ERA, have also been taken to recycling centers, where the glass and metal can be re-used to manufacture electronic games for small children. On the other hand, cultural life is definitely the poorer. As happened in the 1920's, sensitive and creative people have fled the United States to take up residence in Europe, where smoking is still tolerated—even at four or so dollars per pack. Such individuals flaunt their defiance of American provincialism by smoking cigarettes that are 200 mm. in length. And there are always embarrassing international incidents, as when the President of Egypt had his pipe confiscated upon his arrival at Andrews Air Force Base.

Admittedly, this doesn't prove very much of anything. The central issue in the nationwide debate, as everyone remembers, was whether the adoption of the Amendment would make nuclear war more likely or less likely. Opponents of the Amendment had argued that a ban on smoking could easily make crisis situations even less manageable than they had been before. A former Secretary of State, recalling the tense atmosphere in the White House Situation Room during many grave crises, had cautioned against depriving important decision makers of their access to pipes, cigars, and cigarettes. People Against War, an organization which argued not without precedent that peace was better than war most of the time, took a contrary view. They maintained that smoking was just another manifestation of *machismo* which biased the same decision makers toward violent, rather than peaceful, solutions. They pointed out, quite rightly in the view of most historians, that the great age of Western imperialism, born in the sixteenth century, coincided with the introduction of tobacco into Europe. In this regard, much research was also devoted to the relationship between smoking and the appearance of Fascism in Italy. But it was uncertain whether Benito Mussolini took up smoking before or after he became the *Duce*, or whether he even smoked at all. The only evidence, and it is inconclusive, is a small entry in the diary of his private secretary, who recalls seeing the *Duce* with his cheeks puffed out. This was his characteristic pose, of course, but until this diary was discovered, no one realized that the *Duce*'s round cheeks resulted from his penchant for chewing tobacco. No less an authority than Henry Kissinger has reported that the late Chairman Mao was a chain smoker, but anyone who has ever smoked a cigarette of Chinese manufacture finds this impossible to believe.

Another important question is whether the political atmosphere has been poisoned. There is something about a classic political battle of the sort that surrounded the ERA to produce crosscurrents and eddies of bad feeling which swirl around like a vortex inside the body politic, sucking in various pieces of flotsam and jetsam which really don't belong there.

For example, manufacturers of smoking substitutes contributed millions of dollars in support of the Amendment. The chewing gum industry, the confectioners, and the makers of the erasers which adorn yellow ⚹2 pencils cranked up their political action committees. The active role of the chewing gum interests produced a response from civic-minded periodontists. The sugar interests, fearing that the dentists would be bought off by pledges to emphasize the production of sugarless gum, fought back with every weapon at their command. The saccharine interests, fearing a resurgence in sugar usage, also joined the fray. Celery growers had to protect their own position, for it was felt that if it were no longer possible to hold a cigarette when consuming a cocktail, the drinkers might turn to celery stalks. This was all to the benefit of the celery growers of course—if they could reach a *modus vivendi* with the huge carrot-growing concerns in the San Fernando Valley. Yet, as the struggle proceeded, all sides realized that they faced a common enemy—boredom.

The President himself maintained a position of neutrality, more or less. When he was very popular, both sides courted him. It seemed as if he were leaning in favor. Then it seemed as if he were leaning against. But, in the interim, he had become quite unpopular, such that the opponents urged him to come out in favor and the proponents urged him to come out against. Then he became popular again, and positions were once again reversed. This tended to confuse the President, who, predictably, began to waver. Finally, he announced that he would take no position, since the Foreign Crisis required his undivided attention. This had a soothing effect—on all except the foreigners, who always worried whenever they received the undivided attention of any American. Even so, the Amendment was finally ratified. And then a large federal loan guarantee had to be made to Zippo Lighter Company in order to forestall its impending bankruptcy. Unlike other lighter manufacturers, Zippo had not been forward-looking enough to convert to the manufacture of small hand warmers when it still had the chance.

Will it work? The betting is that sooner or later the Amendment will be repealed, but that it will take time. No new consensus has emerged, and families are still bitterly divided. As everyone knows, the President's wife was an ardent supporter of the Amendment, and she sued for divorce when the President adopted his stance of "watchful waiting." This was unprecedented, but the President was philosophical about it. To his friends he would note the observation of a long-forgotten Vice-President, who had also been divorced by his wife after announcing to the world: "A woman is only a woman, but a good cigar is a smoke."

The Great Whale

Captain Ahab stood expressionless on the quarterdeck of the *Pequod* as the crew brought her smartly about. Since entering the mouth of the Potomac River, about 110 miles below Washington, D.C., the ship had been guided by four Coast Guard cutters. Now the *Pequod* was about to tie up at the dock; the escort had served its purpose. Ahab had been summoned to answer to the Federal Whaling Commission for his unrelenting pursuit of the great sea mammals, and he was in a foul mood.

The spring hunt was shaping up as a disaster. A hundred miles out from New Bedford, the *Pequod* had been harassed by dozens of small rowboats, each sporting elaborate pennants condemning whale killers and all their works. They had attempted to parlay with Ahab, to bring him to his senses, to urge him to halt his obsessional stalking of whales. They had engaged him in a serious discussion of the ecological implications of his efforts. They were horrified to discover that he had goods of Japanese manufacture on board, and urged him to cast his Sony cassette player overboard. But Ahab had merely tapped his peg leg on the quarterdeck, striking a pose of studied exasperation.

"You have got to come to grips with this, Ahab," one of them had shouted. "You have to get to the bottom of this. We don't understand you at all."

"Humph," Ahab had replied through his speaking trumpet.

"Tell us," another of them said, "what exactly does the White Whale symbolize for you? Is it a symbol of nature? Are you a Christ figure? What's it all about? We tend to think you are a repressed homosexual, and maybe it's time you came out of the cabin, as it were. God knows, there are hints galore that your ship is rife with pederasty. There's probably something going on with Ishmael and that tattooed cannibal of a harpooner of yours. Let's talk about it."

"Thee are the perverts, not the stout lads of this crew," Ahab shot back. "It is the will of God that we sail the seven seas, hunting whales, bringing home their oil so that the homes of the world can be illuminated. Aye, it's a hard and dangerous course but we shall steer by it!"

"Obviously some kind of manic-depressive," muttered the leader of the Save the Whales flotilla.

Ahab had thought that he had seen the last of those insufferable nuisances, but weeks later he had been found by the Coast Guard. The Friends of the Sperm Whale, Inc., it was explained, had filed a series of complaints with the Federal Whaling Commission, and the *Pequod* had to make way for Washington straightaway so that Ahab could answer for the alleged violations.

"Thee and thy Coast Guard and all thy provisions of law art a pain in the arse," Ahab had shouted, biting off the end of his Cuban cigar, which the Coast Guard then proceeded to confiscate on the grounds that it was contraband. "But thee hath me surrounded and we shall make course for the Capital."

Ahab was surprised by the size of the crowd that had gathered at dockside. The Coalition for a Whale-Filled Environment had turned out in force, with flags, banners, and placards everywhere. The *Pequod*'s gangplank was lowered. It was thoroughly inspected by the harbor master, who pronounced it unsafe for use by a handicapped person. After some delay, a wheelchair was produced so that Ahab could be taken off the ship. The harbor master apologized for the delay, explaining that it was necessary for the Harbor Commission to protect itself from lawsuits, even though it seemed unlikely that Ahab would file suit claiming malfeasance.

By the time Ahab had arrived at the headquarters of the Federal Whaling Commission, the hearing room was filled to overflowing. The Administrative Law Judge who was to act as Hearing Examiner rapped his gavel, opening the proceeding.

"We are going to skip over the long list of unsafe labor practices aboard your ship, Captain," the Hearing Examiner began. "That is a problem for the Occupational and Safety Health Administration in any event. But I must say for the record that I am astounded that, in this day and age, you would chase whales in a ship made out of wood, without a single modern convenience of any kind, without any regard for the welfare of your crew, who, as can be plainly seen, are suffering from every imaginable form of vitamin deficiency. There will be lawsuits aplenty, let me assure you. But we must get to the matter at hand."

A member of the Commission's staff unfurled an enormous map of the world and tacked it to an even larger easel. The map was filled with lines describing the voyages of the *Pequod* over the past thirty years. From the Arctic to the Tropics, from the Antarctic to the Baltic Sea, from the coast of Russia, to the coast of China, to the coast of California, the *Pequod* had been everywhere.

"Now," said the Hearing Examiner, "the record is plain that you have exceeded by far the annual number of voyages permitted in the regulations. But I am puzzled by one thing. You and your ship seem to have spent a disproportionate amount of time in American waters. Here, look at this. In the late forties, you concentrated your efforts off the coast of southern California, then for almost eight years you hover off the coast of Maryland. Then you sail all the way around Cape Horn to prowl the waters near San Diego. Then, for a time, you are found in the waters of Long Island Sound. Afterwards, you move further south. And then the dangerous voyage around the Horn once again. What explains it?"

"I hunt the Great White Whale," Ahab said solemnly, "and I am bound by God until I kill it."

"The Great White Whale?" asked the Hearing Examiner.

"Aye," said the Captain with a quiet nod. "It has become the mission of my life and I cannot turn away from it."

"But we know of no Great White Whale," said the Hearing Examiner.

"How quickly thee hath forgotten," said Ahab with a sigh. "I hunt the great beast of the seas, Moby Dick, aye, Moby Dick Nixon. And I shall not rest until I drive my harpoon into him and he spouts black blood!"

A silence fell over the room.

Finally the Hearing Examiner spoke. "You mean, he's still alive? I thought he had been sent to Davy Jones's locker years ago. I am sure that I had read something about it. Are you sure?"

"Aye," said Ahab, "I am certain of it. As your map so plainly details, I have stalked him for years, and yet he eludeth me somehow. It was not so very long ago that I caught sight of him as we sailed Long Island Sound. It enraged me."

"What was he doing?" asked the Hearing Examiner.

"He was spouting," answered Ahab. "Aye, he spouteth still, and I shall know no peace until he spouteth no more."

"Well," whispered the Commodore of the Save the Whales Flotilla to one of his colleagues, "this certainly puts things in a different light. Why, I had no idea that the old salt was doing God's will all along, just as he had been telling us!"

The Hearing Examiner rapped his gavel for order.

"I must say," he said, "that you are the last of a rare breed, those who pursue the whale Moby Dick. Yes, it was an enterprise of excitement and romance, worthy of the best of us. But it is not as profitable as it once was. Indeed, it is a dead industry. Ah, but what a stirring chapter in American maritime history! It will take a Joseph Conrad to tell it—passion, courage, adventure!" The Hearing Examiner seemed carried away with the wonder of it. "I suppose I meant a Herman Melville, but no matter."

A few more routine questions, and the Hearing Examiner rapped his gavel once again. "These proceedings are adjourned," he said. Then he stood up and told the old whaler that he would accompany him back to his ship.

Twenty minutes later, they were at dockside, standing at the gangplank of the *Pequod*. The Hearing Examiner thrust out his hand. "Good luck and Godspeed, Captain," he said with a slight catch in his voice.

"Aye, that is what we shall need," said the old mariner. "But now that we understand each other, let us not be so formal. Call me Ahab."

Music of the Spheres

Some years ago, in a place some two hours' driving time from Washington, the federal government constructed a vast array of radio telescopes which had, as their purpose, the search for extraterrestrial intelligence. Having soured on the possibilities of normal human intelligence, the authorities had decided to search across the cosmos for an intelligence of a higher type which might unravel the mysteries of stagflation, urban blight, and other problems.

Naturally, it had not been publicly disclosed that contact had been established, for there were instabilities in the bond market which might be aggravated. In fact, there never seemed to be an opportune time to reveal this startling information, so the fact that regular communication was being conducted between ordinary earthlings and a small group of futurologists in a nearby galaxy remained a closely guarded national secret.

As everyone knows, the closest galaxies are really quite far away. A message traveling at the speed of light will take several years to reach its destination. In this particular instance, the distant place in question was a bit less than nine light-years away. Hence, an exchange of messages took slightly less than eighteen years, which was not altogether disheartening, for it closely approximated the amount of time it took for the United States Postal Service to deliver a first-class letter from one borough of New York City to another. The first message sent out by the Americans included an etching of two nude humans, some recorded music, and the full text of the report of the President's Commission on the National Purpose, so that all throughout the cosmos would know where we were going as a people. It included also a brief biography of America's best-known and most revered political figure, Larethan Jerome Wimbol, who, at age one hundred and forty-six, was the oldest man ever to sit in the United States Senate. Of course, Wimbol was much younger when contact was established. He had not yet begun even his seventh term in the Senate, and he was still a Republican, not yet having returned once again to the Democratic Party he had deserted during the Civil War.

From the start, it had been concluded that Senator Wimbol was the only prominent American destined to live long enough to maintain continuity within this unique cosmic communication. Besides, Wimbol was a vast repository of Americana, with a repertoire of political anecdotes and lively gossip which made him an ideal raconteur. And thus it happened that every eighteen years or so, Senator Wimbol would receive a mysterious telephone call, a plain green car would appear in front of his home, and he would be taken to the radio astronomy site to read, and to respond to, the message that was waiting for him.

On this particular Saturday—for Wimbol would never leave on an ordinary working day for fear of offending his constituents—the Senator's phenomenal memory and powerful insight were pressed to their fullest. Years ago, those other sentient

beings out there in the universe had described how their
planet had achieved a degree of complete tranquillity and
prosperity after a series of intricate adjustments in their Central Bank's discount rate. This had led Wimbol, a leading
backer of America's new Federal Reserve System back in
1912, to become a monetarist. They had also described how
their fifth planetary war had been triggered by a struggle over
their planet's dwindling supply of smoked whitefish, leading
Wimbol to become a pioneer in the protection of endangered
species. They had explained how the best minds among them
had avoided speculating about Planetary War III, and had instead moved on directly to speculating about War IV after the
end of War II, on the grounds that a World War III was "ana-
lytically uninteresting." This had led Wimbol to become a
trustee of the Rand Corporation. They had also let it be
known that they had achieved an average life expectancy of
more than three hundred years. Though they had taken to
chiding Wimbol for his immaturity—he was, after all, nothing
but a kid by their reckoning—they were nonetheless impressed
with the Senator's detailed account of surgery that had been
performed on the jaw of President Grover Cleveland, for the
aliens were creatures who did not have jaws. In fact, they did
not talk at all. They communicated by vibrating their ears at
different frequencies, which vibrations were deciphered by
the sensory apparatus of the intended listener. Wimbol had
attempted to employ this technique on the floor of the Senate
in the late 1920's, but it was immediately perceived that communication in this manner would render impossible the
printing publication of the *Congressional Record*.

When Wimbol arrived at the National Center for Radio Astronomy, he introduced himself to the new Director. In the
past eighteen years, the facility had been upgraded and mod-
ernized, and there had been a complete changeover in the
staff. The new Director, who had never met Senator Wimbol
before, was struck by the firm handshake of the near-
sesquicentenarian.

"I have gone through the log of the messages exchanged

with the aliens," said the Director, "and I have been very impressed with the skill you have shown in convincing them that our intentions are peaceful. As you know, at the beginning they thought that the music we were broadcasting to them was a sign of our hostility. I'm glad you explained it to them; you may have helped deter a pre-emptive attack. As long as we keep the lines of communication open, as long as we're talking to each other, we won't be fighting. Indeed, if I may paraphrase that famous remark by Winston Churchill, 'jaw jaw is better than star war, eh, eh.'"

Wimbol winced visibly at this feeble pun on Sir Winston's legendary aphorism. "Ahem," he said, clearing his throat, "I have never thought of my role in this experiment as one of representing Earth as a whole. Rather, I represent myself. These messages have been enormously valuable to me. They have allowed me to get a jump on the issues of the day. I am in fact years ahead of everyone else, which accounts for my startling ability to predict the trend of events, devise new and imaginative solutions, and introduce far-reaching pieces of legislation. I am thus smarter than all the members of my office staff combined. Besides, I am eminently trustworthy. I am hardly about to tell anyone the source of these insights. Not only wouldn't anyone believe me, but I suspect that, in view of my considerable age, the political pressmen would conclude that I had finally become a bit dotty."

The Director, who was nothing but an astrophysicist and radio astronomer with little sense of the inner dynamics of politics, did not know what to make of this. The whole purpose of this expensive enterprise was the betterment of the human race, not the advancement of personal political interests. In truth, he was mightily offended. But his predecessors had somehow found a way to cope with this obvious eccentric, and he would too.

The aliens' message was very long, as had become their custom. Once again, as they had on two occasions since 1912, they still wondered why the Earthlings had not yet mastered the intricacies of the discount rate. As usual, they requested explanations of the strange music which was still being broadcast to them. They also renewed their requests for more etchings of the sort that had been contained in the first message from Earth, especially of nude women. This was a simple task. The astronomers, who had mastered the art of re-creating photographs from faint radio signals, had been preoccupied with reducing the photographs in every issue of *Playboy* to digital radio transmissions, for broadcast into outer space. The aliens had said that theirs was not the only distant planet receiving the photos. They had become popular throughout the Milky Way and some had even made their way to the Crab Nebula in Andromeda. Here, the time lag was less important than in the area of music, for there is a permanence to female beauty, but an evanescence to popular song. Creatures throughout the universe understood that the American music they picked up on their own receivers was just woefully out of date. To this, the American astronomers had replied that the laws of physics decreed that anyone who chose to live outside the Solar System was forever condemned to be behind the times, if not to be totally out of it.

For Wimbol, of course, all this was piffle. His unique ties to the extraterrestrial had always given him a leg up on the issues, and this is what interested him. His advisers in space did not disappoint him. For in the midst of the rather rambling message of the aliens, they did mention in passing the latest research on their planet in the field of carcinogens. They had managed, they said, to eliminate from their biosphere all those agents which contributed to the spread of cancer. Indeed, they had been surprised to discover that among the more dangerous agents were oxygen, chlorophyll, rubber bands, wrapping paper, toothpicks, ultrasuede, felt-tipped pens, shaving cream, heavy water, unlined three-by-five index cards, 35-mm. camera film, and glass marbles. Wimbol resolved to persuade the Congress to ban all of these things in the United States.

The message from the aliens concluded, and they allowed as that it was time for them to sign off for a while, in that it was almost harvest time where they lived and all available hands were needed in the fields. Wimbol, as usual, had assembled some representative abstracts from the American press to transmit into space. He recorded also his latest ruminations about the state of the world and these, too, were transformed into digital radio signals to be beamed across the vast emptiness. There had been some major developments these past eighteen years and it was important that the aliens retain a proper respect for Earth's achievements and proper fear of Earth's ability to hold its own in any interplanetary war. He signed off with this customary closing: "Remember, my friends," he said, "the human adventure has just begun."

The Rocking House Winner

There once was a little boy named Andrew who received a splendid wooden rocking horse for Christmas, beautifully sculptured, with harness, bridle, and saddle all made of genuine Morocco leather. The rocking horse was given to him by his grandfather, the acknowledged dean of the Washington press corps. Andrew spent several hours each day rocking on his horse. Sometimes he would rock very quickly, so quickly that boy and horse were nothing but a blur to concerned onlookers. But after a short period of such rapid rocking, Andrew would come to a sudden stop, dismount, and, with a glazed look in his eye, call out two numbers. They were always three-digit numbers. "Two eighteen, two seventeen," he might say. Or "three oh six, one twenty-nine." But they were always three-digit numbers.

This was curious, and was soon a source of some concern to the boy's parents. Why would the child do such a thing? One day, just before dinner, Andrew mounted his horse, and began to rock faster and faster. His rocking reached a frenzied crescendo, then came to a stop. The boy dismounted and said "one eighty-three, two fifty-two," and was then quiet. About an hour later, the grandfather rang his son to report on a startling development. From his perch in the press gallery, overlooking the House of Representatives, the old man announced the wholly unexpected defeat of the Onion Subsidy Act, not five minutes ago. "An astounding defeat for the President," he said. "All he could muster was one hundred and eighty-three votes, but there were two hundred and fifty-two against him." Totally unexpected, his son had thought as he hung up the phone. And then it came to him. Those numbers were exactly those that Andrew had spoken when he had gotten off his rocking horse, and he had spoken them almost one hour *before* the critical vote had occurred.

It was impossible, so it seemed, and yet it would have been an uncanny coincidence. The boy's father, who had taken to writing down whatever Andrew said after his rides—so as to report on them to the child's psychiatrist—re-examined the notes he had been keeping. Jotting down the numbers of the past week, he consulted back issues of the *Congressional Record* the next morning, and exhaled in amazement. The pattern was unmistakable. Young Andrew had accurately predicted the outcome of every vote cast in the House of Representatives, anywhere from one hour to two days before they had occurred.

The boy's father was not long in coming to an obvious conclusion: "From this kid's gift of prophecy, I could make a good living!"

So the next day, Andrew's father got a list of all votes scheduled for the House of Representatives in the coming week, moved a chair into Andrew's playroom, and waited for him to mount up. The child repeated the ritual. He spoke three sets of numbers, which his father jotted down. Checking them against the legislative schedule, he realized that he now knew the outcome of the next three critical votes that would occur. Stuffing his notes into his pocket, he made for the neighborhood movie theater—where the chief usher was in fact a bookmaker.

"I want to put two hundred dollars down on the Creole Naturalization Act to lose," said Andrew's father to the bookie.

"You what?" answered the bookie in disbelief.

"I said," repeated Andrew's father, "two hundred dollars on the Creole Naturalization Act to lose."

"You mean you want to bet on the vote of a bill that's up in Congress?" asked the bookie.

"The same," said Andrew's father.

"Gee," said the bookie. "I dunno, nobody's ever wanted to bet on that before. I gotta check it out with my people and see if they've got a morning line, if you know what I mean."

"I'll wait," said Andrew's father.

After five minutes or so, the bookie returned. "Well," he said, "I kinda checked it out, and my people say it's O.K." What he had neglected to tell Andrew's father was that his superiors on the other end of the line had checked it out for themselves and, using their impressive contacts among the Creoles, had found out that the bill was a sure winner. "This guy's crazy," the chief had said to his bookie, "but if he wants to throw away his money, we might as well take it. But don't quote him no odds."

Andrew's father returned two days later to collect his winnings, for, just as young Andrew had indicated, the Creole Naturalization Act had been defeated, and by precisely the margin of fifty-one votes the child had predicted.

"I feel hot today," said Andrew's father, counting his money, "and I'm ready to take a big plunge. I will put a thousand dollars on the Vanilla Extract Act to pass."

"Gee, I dunno if we can handle that kind of action," said the bookie, "but I'll check."

Once again, the bookie telephoned his chief, who was even less concerned than he was the first time. "Ah, this guy just got lucky," he said. "Look, one thing people in our line of

work know about is dangerous drugs, and there ain't twenty
votes in the Congress to have vanilla extract declared a dangerous drug. You can count on it. Believe me, we've done our
work on this one and we've spread a lot of money around."

"Fine by me," the bookie answered, and he returned to in-
form Andrew's father that the bet would be taken. But following the suggestion of the chief, he decided that the bookmak-
ing operation's previous losses could be recouped if Andrew's
father could be persuaded to wager even more on the outcome of the vote on vanilla extract.

"Tell you what," the bookie said, "you put down five thousand on this one, and we'll give you eight-to-one odds. You a
man or a mouse?"

"Wonderful," said Andrew's father, and he agreed.

Naturally, the bookie was severely shaken when, on the following day, he was obliged to pay out forty thousand dollars.
For once again, the child's predictions had been unerring. The
bill declaring vanilla extract a controlled substance had
passed by a huge margin, one hundred and eleven votes, just
as the boy had indicated.

Thus it had begun, and so it continued. The child would
descend from his rocking horse, the father would note the
numbers, the bookie would accept the bets, and the winnings
of Andrew's father reached a staggering sum.

But as could have been predicted, word of these developments could not be contained. Bookies around the city heard
that one of their colleagues was sustaining huge losses to
someone who wagered on the outcome of legislative votes.
Their customers also got wind of it and, fairly soon, there was
an active business in wagering on these contests. Of course,
Andrew's father was the only consistent winner and, on the
whole, the bookmakers were turning a tidy profit on this new
gambling craze in the Nation's Capital.

A turning point was reached when the local newspapers got
wind of it and began to list not only the bills that would be
voted upon on a particular day, but the "vote spread" that had

been established for them in Las Vegas. Thus, for example, one could read that the Pest Control Cartel Deregulation Act would be voted upon Tuesday afternoon, and that it was favored to pass by eleven and a half votes. As in football, the important thing was to beat the spread, not necessarily to predict the winner. It also became known that the congressmen themselves were among the most vigorous wagerers; it was soon suggested that some congressmen were casting their votes in accordance with how they had wagered on the outcome. This was a wholly new development. Fortunes were won and lost. A new consulting industry sprang into being. Dope sheets were published, and the best of these, "Morning Legislative Line," soon had an impressive circulation. One unfortunate legislator was barred from organized politics for life by the Commissioner when it was discovered that the fellow was a habitual wagerer on votes in which he had participated. "The fans must have confidence in the integrity of the legislative game," the Commissioner had said somberly after announcing his controversial decision.

But none of this affected Andrew and his father in the slightest. They did not deviate from their routine. The child would speak his numbers and his father would place his bets. His winnings were awesome.

Understanding the limitless possibilities of this arrangement, Andrew's father had, from the start, said not one word about it to Andrew's mother. The truth was that Andrew's father could now afford to indulge in proclivities and tastes which had been long suppressed because of the family's tight budget. Besides, the mother of the house might tip off someone and, with the secret revealed, the game would be over.

And yet, in the intervening months, Andrew's mother had become ever more concerned. The father, who had considered his son something of a dolt, now took an obsessive interest in his well-being. He would bring home enormous stuffed animals for the child; he bought him electric trains; he allowed him to eat as many pieces of saltwater taffy as the youngster's heart desired. He could stay up as late as he wanted, and his father allowed the boy to stay home from school whenever he expressed the desire.

When Andrew's mother spoke of these developments during her weekly visits to the child's psychiatrist, the physician seemed unconcerned. He had, he said, worked out an explanation for the child's compulsive rocking on the horse. "Merely a way of gaining the father's attention," he had opined. "Just another stage in his psychosexual development bound to pass sooner or later."

So it was not surprising that the relationship between Andrew and his horse changed abruptly. One day, as Andrew was in the midst of furious rocking, he rocked altogether too vigorously, and found himself thrown from the horse onto the floor. Young Andrew became enraged. He ran to the tool shed and returned with a hatchet. He began hacking away at what was formerly his favorite toy until he had reduced it to a pile of slivers. When his father returned that evening, Andrew pointed to the mess on the playroom floor and said to his father, "Wrap up this splintered nag and send him back to Grandpa."

"Isn't it wonderful!" Andrew's mother exclaimed. "The child has ended his obsessive attachment to that silly horse."

But Andrew's father had heard none of it. The sight alone had caused him to collapse on the floor. He never regained consciousness, and his passing was little noticed in the community. His vast hoard of cash was never discovered.

"Oh, well," said Andrew to his old and ragged teddy bear, "you can keep whispering those numbers in my ear. I guess I'll never understand why Horsie would get so worked up whenever I would repeat them to him."

Entertainment

For the brilliance and luster of social gatherings, for the fun and excitement of parties, there was not an embassy in Washington which had rivaled that of the Republic of Pâté. In fact, the dominance of the Embassy of Pâté on the social scene had illustrated how planning, tact, and financial resources could make the outpost of even the tiniest country a dominant force in the Nation's Capital. For intrinsically speaking, of course, the Republic of Pâté had been an insignificant place, even by today's standards of nationhood. In fact, it had gained its independence only as something of an afterthought. It was, as one observer put it, nothing but a small bite of country sandwiched between two larger crackers on the coast of South America. It had been Belgium's only holding in the New World, and it would have received independence in the early 1960's if someone had only remembered to grant it. But it was not freed, or admitted to the United Nations, until 1974.

One would have thought that it would have adopted a new name upon independence. But the only transition was that between its status as Enclave and Republic. Its unusual name springs from the first reactions of the Belgian explorers who discovered the place. The beaches of Pâté are noted for their gooey consistency, and the first Belgian who strode ashore centuries ago is believed to have remarked that the beach had the consistency of goose liver. This fact explains not merely the Republic's name, but the more important fact—namely, that a tourist industry has never flourished there.

But none of this mattered very much. In an age when natural resources are said to account for the power of countries in the Third World, the emergence of Pâté had belied that generalization. Pâté possessed but one natural resource, a charming and handsome Ambassador, and that is what made the difference. He quickly grasped the essence of the diplomatic circuit, which is to say that if you invite people they'll come.

He invited the offensive line of the Pittsburgh Steelers, and they came. He invited every member of the College of Cardinals, and they came. He invited the Executive Council of the Irish Republican Army, and they came. He invited everyone who had ever received an award from the Country Music Association of America, and they came. He invited every member of the Concertgebouw orchestra in Amsterdam, and they came. He invited all of the extras who had appeared in the film *Ben Hur*, and they came. He invited all members of the Royal Canadian Mounted Police who had ever served in the Yukon, and they came. He invited all those who had won prizes in the Connecticut lottery, and they came. He invited the membership of the Crimean War Veterans Descendants Organization, and they came. He invited Leonid Brezhnev's ex-mistress, and she came. He invited the Vienna Boys Choir, and they came. He invited every dog that had been awarded a ribbon by the Westminster Kennel Club, and they came. He invited everyone who had ever committed perjury before a congressional committee, and they came. He invited the labor representative of the Professional Jai Alai Players Association, and he came—even though he had received death threats from a Basque terrorist organization.

He invited the stewards at Epsom Downs, and they came. He invited all the blackjack dealers in Atlantic City, and they came. He invited all the chefs in the province of Szechwan, and they came; they even brought their own food with them. He invited every matador who had killed more than one hundred bulls, and they came. He invited all the meteorologists stationed in Antarctica, and they came. He invited the inventor of the legal pad, and she came. He invited everyone who had ever received a score of 800 on a College Entrance Examination Board test, and they came. He invited every member of Alcoholics Anonymous, but the invitations were undeliverable. He invited the faculty of the Department of Plant Genetics at Kansas State University, and they came. He invited all exiled Cuban cigar makers, and they came. He invited Charles Revson, the cosmetics magnate, and Charles Ronson, the cigarette-lighter magnate, but both invitations were mistakenly delivered to Charles Bronson, the actor, who came in their stead. He invited Charles Bronson on his own account, but his invitation was mistakenly delivered to Edgar Bronfman.

He invited Jacqueline Bouvier Kennedy Onassis, but the invitation was returned marked "addressor unknown." He invited everyone who had purchased a copy of *Thy Neighbor's Wife*, and they came. He invited the members of the House of Keys on the Isle of Man, and they came. He invited the motormen who operated the East Side line of the IRT, and they came. He invited the members of every Soviet spy ring in Britain, and they came. He invited everyone who had ever attended an auction at Sotheby's, and they came. He invited all those who had had their radial tires recalled, and they came. He invited everyone who had ever survived a Big Mac Attack, and they came. He invited everyone who hated digital watches, and they came. He invited everyone who believed that the scientists who worked for *Consumer Reports* were actually receiving secret payoffs from manufacturers, and they came. He invited every scientist who worked for *Consumer Reports,* and they came and rated the chemical purity of the potato-chip dip. He invited everyone who smoked Balakan Sobranie cigarettes, and they came. He invited everyone who had ever tripped over the extra-long cord of a Princess telephone, and they came. He invited everyone who had ever written a doctoral dissertation about James Joyce, and they came. He invited everyone who had ever written a doctoral dissertation on William Faulkner, and they came, and they argued with those who had written about Joyce. He invited all Mormons who lived in the state of West Virginia, and they came. He invited anyone who had broken a bone during the most recent skiing season, and they came. He invited every dentist who owned a Mercedes-Benz, and they came. He invited everyone who had ever been caught smoking in the non-smoking section of a passenger airplane, and they came. He invited everyone who had ever purchased oil on the spot market, and they came. He invited everyone who knew what the spot market was, and no one came. He invited all Washington Redskins season ticket holders, and they came. He invited all of the Muppets, and even they came. In fact, the only people who never showed up were the gnomes of Zurich, who never accept any invitations. It is their policy.

The reason that everyone came whenever invited was that the food was exceptionally good, the conversation stimulating, and stories about the parties appeared in many newspapers. For those who especially valued entertainment at parties, the Ambassador always took the precaution of inviting an opera company, which could always be persuaded to stage a complete production. Sometimes, the main ballroom was darkened and popular films were shown. Frequently, there were cockfights on the lawn of the Embassy. There was always Muzak in the Embassy's powder rooms. Guests were always allowed to slide down the marble banister of the main staircase, where they had the pleasant experience of landing in a huge tub of lime Jell-O. The Embassy was situated next to twenty-three acres of woodland, and big game hunts were organized. Sometimes, during intermissions in the operatic productions, karate demonstrations were staged, though these were abandoned after a drunken guest wandered into the midst of one and was split in two. A high wire was strung diagonally from one corner of the main ballroom to the other, and acrobats carrying long balancing poles walked about overhead; sometimes, one of them would ride a small motorcycle on the wire. An oil-drilling rig was kept in constant operation on the front lawn, so that people might observe one in action, but even at a depth of 14,000 feet, no oil had been discovered. (It had been the Ambassador's fondest dream to bring in a gusher during one of his parties, so that the guests could leave having been spattered with black gold.)

The Mayor of the Capital was driven to proclaim a one-week mourning period after the Revolution came to Pâté. The new crew was a sullen bunch and went so far as to recall the Ambassador. They removed the tightrope and turned off the oil rig. They did not, however, know what to do with the tub of Jell-O, because they had never seen one, and kept it in its customary place as an object of veneration. But they stopped inviting everyone, so no one came. The former Ambassador had the good sense not to return home. Instead, he became a naturalized citizen of the new Island Republic of Guano, and was soon appointed that Republic's Ambassador to the United States. The Guanese, equally intent upon acquiring influence, encouraged him to resume business as usual. The parties are now better than ever. "It is wrong," the Ambassador said when he presented his credentials, "to assume that all stories have an unhappy ending."

Genealogy

As part of its continuing study of the American heritage, the Smithsonian Institution recently dispatched its chief genealogist to interview the oldest Jewish woman in Silver Spring, Maryland, on the occasion of her ninety-sixth birthday. The transcript of the interview, as published in *Smithsonian* magazine, created no small sensation. Indeed, many believe that the interview was a principal cause of the communal violence which recently racked the Nation's Capital:

"Well, Mrs. Gordon, you're ninety-six years old and a priceless historical resource. You must tell me everything you remember about the old country so the Smithsonian Institution can trace your family tree."

"What's to remember? In Minsk, everything was terrible! I could tell you stories about pogroms that would curl your hair. Don't forget, we had the Tsar in Minsk, and no Anti-Defamation League to take full-page ads. It's better not even to remember it, it was so terrible."

"We don't need to dwell on unpleasant memories. Why don't you just tell me how your family came to be established in America."

"We came by boat."

"By boat?"

"What then? What should we come by, the *Hindenburg?*"

"Tell me, Mrs. Gordon, what was daily life like in Minsk? Do you remember your own mother? What was she like?"

"My mother died when I was very young. I was raised by my great-aunt, my *tante.* We called her Tante Tinte; she was a saint, a true saint. *Ach,* what would have happened to me without Tante Tinte?"

"So you don't remember your mother; what about your grandmother?"

"My grandmother was a whole different story altogether! First of all, she was well-to-do, comfortable, if you know what I mean. Grandfather had made a lot of money in woolens, what you would call today the garment trade. Of course, in those days they didn't have synthetics or permanent-pressed with Dacron; they had only woolens. Some cotton too, but mostly woolens. He made more than a good living. Every winter, the family would go to the Crimea where it was warmer—sometimes even to Italy or the Greek islands. To return to Minsk in those days with a suntan was some big deal, you should know that. The sunlamp hadn't been invented, so a tan then was the real thing."

"So your grandmother was a powerful figure in your family."

"Powerful is the right word, you should believe it. She was in charge of everything. She ran a big household, always with entertaining, especially on the holidays. And that was no easy job in those days. We hadn't then what you call now labor-saving devices like they give away on the daytime quiz shows. Electricity, even, there wasn't!"

"How did she manage?"

"Manage? She had help. What else?"

"What do you mean by help?"

"Well, it's one of the great memories of my childhood, going to my grandmother's house after she got help. I remember how she used to complain and complain, how you couldn't get a reliable girl to come in to clean, how they were always stealing things or not showing up, especially when you needed them. For hours and hours my grandmother would go on about how you couldn't get reliable help. But she finally got it all worked out."

"How did it happen?"

"I don't remember the details, but I remember that the problem was solved after they bought Lilly."

"Bought Lilly? What is Lilly?"

"Not what, who! You should know the truth that today Lilly was what you would call an Afro-American, but then they had a Yiddish word which I won't use because you'll think it's not polite. Anyway, Lilly was what you would call today a minority."

"You mean she was a black?"

"I'm not saying; you'll have to draw your own conclusions. It's not nice to talk about these things anyway. It's almost ninety years ago when I was six years old and my grandmother then was already at least eighty-seven when she was telling me what it was like after she had reliable help, so it's a long time ago we are talking, believe me."

"What was Lilly's last name?"

"Who can remember each and every little detail? I do remember that my grandmother said that Lilly was not her real name. It's terrible to talk about it now, but they had bought Lilly from a dealer in minorities. I think my grandmother was the first person in that part of Russia to have minority help. But it caught on very fast, though it never became as fashionable as owning your own serf. I think maybe the Jews were not allowed to own serfs; maybe they were serfs. It's all very confusing."

"Did you ever meet Lilly?"

"I think maybe I did meet her, when she was about to re-tire. She talked about going to a place called the New World, which I thought was a retirement place with condominiums, like leisure village. But I think she wanted to go to South Car-olina, which must have been a terrible place before they built Hilton Head."

"So you lost track of Lilly?"

"I think she used to write every once in a while from the New World to tell my grandmother how things were going and how she had found some long-lost relatives there. Ah, yes, I remember my grandmother once told me that Lilly had come to Minsk from someplace in Africa with an Italian name like *bambina*."

"Gambia! Could it have been the Gambia?"

"I think that's right, but who can remember after all these years."

"Then she went to Minsk and then to South Carolina?"

"Not only to South Carolina, but all over! Believe me, life wasn't easy in those days. You young people don't appreciate the advantages you have today."

"This is absolutely amazing, totally and completely amazing! Do you realize what you are saying?"

"What are you talking?"

"I'm talking about the woman known to you as Lilly. Don't you realize it all fits?"

"What does it fit?"

"You mean you didn't watch *Roots* on television?"

"I didn't see, but I've read. What else is there to read about except *Roots?*"

"Don't you see, Mrs. Gordon? Your grandmother's cleaning woman back in Minsk was Alex Haley's great-great-great-grandmother!"

"Alex Haley, the writer from *Roots?* You mean we are re-lated? Who could even imagine such a thing!"

"It is remarkable, Mrs. Gordon, that your grandmother's

cleaning woman's great-great-great-grandson would grow up to be Alex Haley! What do you think about that?"

"Well, this is America after all. What else can you expect?"

"But this is staggering, Mrs. Gordon! I've stumbled upon the genealogical discovery of the century! To be able to trace Alex Haley's origins to Minsk will have a revolutionary impact on the study of genealogy in this country!"

"You shouldn't get so excited, you should pardon me for saying. It's up the wrong tree you are probably barking. If you'll excuse me for saying, I don't think it's so likely. It's a one-in-a-million chance. How should I tell you, it's a touchy subject, but so many colored in Minsk there weren't, I can assure you. Even a Jew had to be a little crazy to live there, if you understand me. And the winters! They didn't have a sun belt in Russia."

"Mrs. Gordon, maybe you have some other relatives who can give some additional information to help me confirm this epoch-making hypothesis of mine. Please try to remember. It's very important."

"You'll calm down for a moment and let me think. Well, there are some others of my family who came to America you could probably find."

"Who are they and where do they live?"

"It's a complicated story. You remember I told you from my wonderful great-aunt, Tante Tinte. We don't like to talk about it, but Tante Tinte had a sister, also my great-aunt, Tante Yotashevska, who for short we just called Tante Yo. It's such a tragedy, you don't even want to hear it."

"No, it's very important that I know, so please try to recall as much as you can."

"If the truth be told, and God forgive me for talking about it, Tante Yo got into some trouble with a rabbinical student who lived not so far away. She was in what we used to call the family way. Her father, also a dealer in woolens, was very angry, so angry he threw her out of the house, and told her never to come back."

"Where did she go?"

"Go? To America, where everyone went, she and her little son, descended from generations of rabbis and scholars. She went somewhere to the Wild West, to the Great Plains, someplace called Namota."

"Namota? Are you sure? Could it be Dakota?"

"Namota. Dakota. Who's arguing? There were two of these Namota places, my son once told me, a north and a south, but I forget which one it was. Maybe she went to both. Probably, it was South Namota—you'll pardon me—South Dakota, where I think it is a little warmer."

"What did she do when she got there?"

"You must promise never to tell anyone. Something like this never happened in our family, not for generations, I swear to you, so you'll have to keep this, how do you say it, off the record."

"We will protect your great-aunt's memory, don't you worry."

"It's been so long, someone might as well know. Tante Yo married with an Indian, a real Wild West one, but from the tribe that is having the hole in their noses, whatever they're called."

"The Nez Perce?"

"Pinz Nez, Nez Pince, Nez Perce, what do I know? And they had a son who, to keep alive the tradition, they named Joseph, after the one who led the Jews into Egypt. With such a background, well, Joseph was a smart boy. He really applied himself. When he grew up, he became chief of all the Indians with the holes in their noses, the Pierced Schnozz, or whatever you call them."

"You must mean the famous Chief Joseph of the Nez Perce! This is more astounding still! If what you are telling me is correct, Chief Joseph was half Jewish."

"Wrong altogether. All Jewish. If you know the Talmud, you know it's the *mothers* what is making the *kind* Jewish or not."

"Mrs. Gordon, if I can document this, I will become the

most famous genealogist in America. I will become the Curator of the Smithsonian's Museum of Ethnological History. I will have it made!"

"I think you're getting carried away by yourself again, if you don't mind my saying. After all, Chief Joseph was the black buffalo of the family, I suppose you would say. His mother didn't want him to go into politics, such a dirty business it is. His brother Sidney *really* made something of himself. It's Sidney you should study, not Joseph. Sidney had a lot of his grandfather in him. He used to do some peddling during the buffalo hunts—a little cloth, a little firewater he would import from Bronfman in Canada, things like that. And from this, he built up the biggest dry-goods discount chain in the Black Hills. That already is something, a wonderful story that someone could even write a book about."

"Mrs. Gordon, I don't mean for one moment to denigrate the achievements of Sidney, but that, after all, is genealogically uninteresting. But to establish the Jewish ancestry of Chief Joseph would really be a feather in my cap. Can't you give me some more help?"

"Listen, my young friend, all the evidence you need is already right under your nose, you'll forgive me, it's so simple. I am surprised nobody ever noticed it before, so out in the open is it. But me, I keep my mouth shut out of respect for my family."

"What do you mean?"

"Even I know Chief Joseph was a famous man who said once a famous thing what everyone remembers. You are remembering?"

"Yes. He said, 'I shall fight no more forever.'"

"So you'll tell me, Mr. Genealogist from the Smithsonian: *English like that, where else did he learn it?*"

Sport

At the beginning, the devoted fans of Washington's hockey team did not know what to think when the players appeared on the ice wearing gas masks. Perhaps the masks served no purpose other than to make the team appear more fearsome and intimidating. Some of the spectators had speculated that the masks were but a simple precaution. After all, the last home game had ended in a tumultuous riot, and the police were forced to fire dozens of rounds of tear gas just to clear the arena. Yes, the fans were a demonstrative bunch and it was just common sense to take some simple precautions against mass exuberance.

But it was none of these things. The purpose of the masks did not become apparent until midway in the third period when, trailing six goals to none, the home team began its comeback. Their hockey sticks began to emit a strange substance and, as the vaporous cloud spread, it was obvious that

the visitors were becoming disoriented. In less than two minutes, they had collapsed altogether, allowing the Washington
team to score nine goals in rapid succession. It was the first
known instance of the use of chemical warfare in an officially
sanctioned National Hockey League game, and it was a
striking success.

The Washington coach laid it on the line during a post-
game television interview. "What's the use of playing within a
stone's throw of the Army's chemical warfare research center
if you can't make use of the latest military technology when
the chips are down?" he had asked. "The guys over there are
great fans, real aficionados of the rink, and when they first
came to me with their idea, I was a little skeptical. But we
searched the rule book, and we couldn't find anything which
prohibited it. So what the hell. Look, there will be a lot of
sportswriters who are going to call this a dangerous escalation, but the way I think about it, chemical agents really make
ice hockey more humane. *Mon ami,* if you rely only on the
sticks to go after the other team, there's going to be blood and
pain and an occasional fistfight. This way, nobody suffers. You
lay a whiff of that stuff on them, and that's that. Frankly, I'll
never figure out that bunch of sissies. First they want to ban
the game because it's too gory, then they criticize us for making it more humane."

Of course, there was a certain logic to the coach's position.
Some suspected a case of sour grapes when the losers complained to the League's officials, protesting the use of chemical agents on the ice. Washington's owner had dismissed the
beef with a wave of his hand. "They don't even know when
they're well off," he had said. "What we used the other day
just knocked them out cold for a few minutes. But if we have
to get really rough, we will. We've got stuff that will plain kill
them, and we won't be afraid to use it if we have to."

This was pretty rough talk from a team which had habit-
ually finished the season in the League cellar. But it had its
effect. After all, this was not a bluff very easily called. The

League officials favored some sort of negotiated arrangement, fearing that the game would lose its popular appeal if it became nothing but a contest emphasizing poison gases and their antidotes. What would happen to the speed, the grace, the bodily contact, the French obscenities? It was promised that the issue would be resolved during the off season, and it was. An elaborate face-saving formula was devised, having to do with the safety of the spectators. There thus came into being the Canadian-American Convention on the Employment of Disabling Agents in Professional Ice Hockey, the French and English texts of which were equally authentic.

But that episode had already produced its side effects. The Chief of Staff of the Army, an avid basketball fan—he had captained the West Point five back in the late forties—had made available to the local professional team the latest in the Army's anti-missile technology. Once again, a check of the rule book turned up no inhibitions on its use. The system consisted of several portable laser-beam generators and their associated radars and computers. Easily installed in the rafters of the arena, the system provided an unusually effective defense of the home team's hoop. In fact, more than 70 percent of the visiting team's field goal attempts were knocked down short of the basket. The Free Throw Kill Index was even higher—.879. "It's like having the equivalent of a nine-foot center," the coach had grinned. Indeed, for the very first time in the history of the National Basketball Association, Washington led the league in blocked shots.

But there was a drawback. It was soon discovered that this particular defense—known around the League as the zapping zone—was not cost-effective. The intense heat generated by the lasers vaporized the basketball as it arched toward the basket. Opposing teams began to barrage the system with shots from the floor. In the course of a game, several gross of basketballs might disappear into the realm of anti-matter. League rules required that all balls be provided by the home team. As the cost was projected over the course of an entire season, including the playoffs—which always went on almost

interminably for some reason—the total cost would be astronomical. With the greatest reluctance, the team's president
asked the Army to dismantle its defense system, something it
had become used to doing in any event.

The local baseball team, through this period of scientific advance, had come under severe criticism for its resistance to
modernization. The letters column of *Aviation Week and
Space Technology* was filled with communications from engi-
neers in California describing the latest miracles which might
easily add interest to the nation's pastime. Baseball, as we
know, is resistant to innovation. Even so, the team's fans were
pleased to discover various new devices developed by the Air
Force newly installed in the old baseball stadium. There was,
first of all, the Fly Ball Control System (FLABALSYS). This
was an intricate network of micro-radars which tracked the
course of each fly ball, computed its trajectory, and aimed a
bright light on that point on the field where the ball was certain to descend. This was of great assistance to outfielders.

Infielders had the advantage of the Ground Ball Stress
Analysis Machine (GROBSAM), a matrix of sensing devices
installed under the diamond which instantaneously evaluated
whether a ground ball should be taken on the big hop or the
short hop. Batting averages, overall, rose by more than forty-
seven points, with the use of new bats containing cores made
of ionized metallic hydrogen. These were effective, but risky,
since they sometimes exploded upon contact with the baseball. Equally unpredictable was the "smart ball," developed
by the Air Force's Jet Propulsion Laboratory in Pasadena.
This ingenious device looked exactly like the old-fashioned
horsehide. But its insides included an intricate electronic device, drawing its energy from the sun and therefore not usable
in night games, which permitted the ball, after being pitched,
to home in on the brain waves of the batter. Batters could
thus be beaned with regularity. But it turned out that the
"smart ball" was too vulnerable to jamming. Simple countermeasures could cause the ball to veer off from the batter's
head, and to break low and outside, or to break abruptly

downward, so as to bounce in front of the plate. Though the Washington "smart ball" took an encouraging toll of opposition batters around the League, it caused all too many wild pitches. The research team which had designed the revolutionary spheroid was much embarrassed. An audit revealed there had also been cost overruns.

Interservice rivalry being what it is, the Chief of Naval Operations berated his subordinates for their failure to have an impact on competitive athletics. The Naval Research Laboratory was instructed to turn its attention to water sports. But the results were disappointing. Scuba diving is not a team sport, and not competitive. Nuclear-powered speedboats were unaffordable, even to the richest of sportsmen who raced hydroplanes. True, some refinements were achieved in the water ski after a crash program of tests of new designs was concluded in the Navy's tanks. But these things were trivial. Some thought that the establishment of a North American Water Polo League would stimulate research and development, but the requisite financial backing could not be found. The slogan "The Battle of Leyte Gulf Was Won in the Swimming Pools of Annapolis" never really caught on.

The bad feeling among the armed services intensified. The Secretary of Defense ordered a study of the impact on the annual Army-Navy game if the present trend in the refinement of athletic competition were extrapolated. The assignment was given to the War Gaming Section, which predicted that by 1997 casualties on both sides would exceed 3,000. Armed with this data, the Secretary was able to make a convincing case that future athletic competition among the services academies—in all sports, of course—would lead to the obliteration of the professional officer corps by the end of the century. This was unacceptable.

Cease-and-desist orders were issued, and in the nick of time, for not three days before the upcoming Army-Navy game, copies of the Army game plan fell into the hands of the press. Because the game plan was classified, its contents cannot be revealed here without causing the publisher to absorb enormous court costs. But the fact that forty-one helicopters were assigned to medical evacuation duty suggests the scale of the operations contemplated. As the Point's superintendent remarked, "This ain't beanbag."

Wimbol in Nighttown

     Senator Wimbol had begun the project not merely out of concern for the personal difficulties of his colleagues but out of his deep desire to restore lagging public confidence in the Institution. In truth, during his long service in the Senate, Wimbol had noticed a decline in standards of personal conduct. And when the amorous adventures of Congressman P—— were finally revealed in the most embarrassing way, Wimbol decided to move. "Our weekly prayer breakfast hasn't worked," he said. "Oh, it's all right for the goody-goodies, but doesn't do much for the man who needs help."

Thus Wimbol was led to found the nationwide organization Adulterers Anonymous, with himself as president of the chapter holding Charter Number One, which met weekly in a small house not far from the Supreme Court Building. Here, powerful government figures and well-known private citizens, on a first-name, wholly anonymous basis, would meet over coffee and sandwiches, and grapple with the pressures of modern life. But even Wimbol, in his long experience—for he was, after all, a man who thought he had seen everything—soon realized that this, too, was inadequate. Thus he encouraged friends to establish three other fraternal organizations—Sybarites Pseudonymous, Sodomists Synonymous, and Pederasts Eponymous. All four met together on a monthly basis.

The case of the aforementioned Congressman P—— was especially tragic. As he drifted into middle age, the legislator found that he could achieve sexual fulfillment only in the room atop the Washington Monument, the nation's foremost phallic symbol. He had maneuvered for years to obtain a seat on the House Parks Committee, so as to become chairman of its subcommittee on monuments. In that position, he was entitled, *ex officio*, to a key to the famous obelisk. In truth, many of his lady friends were turned on by the sheer novelty of his preferred trysting place. But on that memorable night when he lured an airline stewardess he had met on the Washington–New York shuttle to the monument grounds, ostensibly to offer her a spectacular view of the Capitol by starlight, tragedy struck. For the stewardess was a well-raised girl, and began to run down the steps of the monument rather than succumb to his advances. He pursued her for more than five hundred steps, but suffered his fatal heart attack at about step 571. (A small plaque now marks the spot.) The incident was immortalized by more than the founding of Chapter One of Adulterers Anonymous, for it figured prominently in a pamphlet the group had printed, prepared by a rake of a professor of moral philosophy at a nearby university, and entitled (as we all know) "The Varieties of Adulterous Experience."

It was at the fifth meeting of the "real AA," as the group came to be known, that Undersecretary R—— acknowledged that he was the "mysterious vandal" who had broken into the house of the giant pandas at the National Zoological Park. The Undersecretary admitted that his only real sensual pleasure in life was to chew on eucalyptus leaves and roll contentedly about, every so often caressing Ling-ling. "But it never got any further than that," he said. "For years, I tried to import a giant panda of my own from the People's Republic of China, and I thought that the normalization of relations between our two countries would finally make it possible for me to get one. God knows, the last thing I had on my mind was destruction of government property or—worse yet—frightening the little bear. When I read that Ling-ling seemed so traumatized by the break-in that she might never conceive, it almost broke my heart." At this point, his narrative dissolved into heartfelt sobs, but he summoned up the courage to continue. "I love the Department, and I love my wife, and I love my children by my wife's first marriage who live with us, and I love my own children by my own first marriage who live with my wife and her second husband, and with his children by his first marriage, whom I also love."

His fellows consoled him, especially Judge B——, who announced that the Undersecretary's courage had helped him find his own. "I know what he's talking about," he said, fighting back tears of his own. "When I collect my scuba gear, my aqualung and my wet suit and my waterproof watch and my waterproof camera and my waterproof flashlight, my wife thinks I'm going off for some especially adventurous nighttime diving. Oh, God, if only she knew the awful truth, if only she knew that she was half right. But I'm in the grip of a powerful compulsion I can't resist. At least twice a month, I sneak into the National Aquarium, don my diving gear, and climb into one of the tanks—it's always the same tank, in fact, tank number 107. This has been going on for nine years, for nine terrible years this constant fear of drowning or disclosure." His head sank into his hands. "I need a towel to dry off," he said.

"I mean," said the Judge, "it all began so innocently, I didn't want to do it, but I couldn't help myself after a while. I just couldn't help myself. I had restrained myself for the longest time, I resisted as long as I could. Now it's been almost nine years, nine years, my God, for nine long years, I've been—I've been get—I mean, I can hardly bring myself to admit it, but for almost nine years, *I've been getting it on with a grouper!*"

"Jiminy Crickets," said Wimbol with a faint whistle. "Getting it on with a grouper? Man, that is heavy, that is just plain far out."

"It's not far out," said the Judge solemnly, "it's just deep down, if you know what I mean."

The group agreed that the Judge definitely needed professional counseling, as his situation was beyond the expertise of anyone present. Then they fell silent, and decided to adjourn.

"I don't know how to begin," said Wimbol when the group next reconvened. "This is a happy day. I can report that our brother the Judge has taken our advice to heart, and has not been in the tank since our last meeting. True enough, he has taken to standing outside the tank, along with the tourists, staring longingly, but the crisis has passed. He's over that infatuation at last." The Judge acknowledged the approving murmurs of his colleagues.

"But now," continued Wimbol, "our comrade the Agency Director has come to us with another problem, which he has discussed with me, but which I have persuaded him he must share with the group."

The poor Director. He betrayed a nervousness that none had ever witnessed before. "Brothers," he said, "you have helped me find my courage too. In fact, I don't know how I could have survived this ordeal without you. It's the kind of thing you can't share with your friends in the neighborhood, or even with your in-laws. How did it start? How do any of these things start? It was spring, ten years ago, and, as I always did, I helped my son plant a small vegetable garden in our backyard. But that year, it was different. I mean, it was the strangest thing, the odd sensation that came over me as I handled the soil, pulled the weeds, poured out the pine-bark mulch. I hadn't felt like that since I was fifteen. I guess I had just been struggling against my own nature, bottling it up inside, denying it to myself. But I realized then that I could no longer contain it. I faced the brutal fact. I was a hortosexual."

"A hortosexual?" inquired the City Councilman. "What's that?"

"A hortosexual," said the Director, "is a male or a female with an affectional preference for plants, either fruits or vegetables."

"I ain't never heard of that before in all my life; that sure as hell is one my pappy never told me about, for damn sure," gasped the prominent automobile dealer.

"It's not all that unusual," said the Director. "I mean, we are well organized; we have our own group based in California, where all this got started. It's called the Luther Burbank Society. Our motto is 'Love 'em and harvest 'em!'"

"Let the man get on with his story," said Wimbol. "Those who haven't done the assigned reading before the monthly meetings are just going to have a hard time following the discussion." And with that, the Director resumed.

"Yes," said the Director, "I had discovered my true nature, but I was afraid to reveal it to my wife, who, if the truth be told, had often called me a fruit, not even guessing how close she was to the bitter truth. I began to prowl the National Arboretum by night carrying a copy of Roger Tory Peterson's *The Hortosexual's Complete Field Guide to Consenting Shrubs of the Middle Atlantic Region,* flitting aimlessly, purposelessly, never developing meaningful relationships. And then winter would come, and it was simply too cold to stay outdoors at night. I had to find another haunt. In a flash, it came to me—the Botanical Garden at the foot of the United States Capitol, with temperature and humidity carefully controlled, and with a bewildering variety of floral!"

The Director took a long swallow from his coffee cup, and then continued. "I used to sneak into the Botanical Garden at night. The security there was very weak. First it was once or twice a month, then once a week, then almost every night. I couldn't get enough. But to give oneself over to one's hortosexuality is to open the way to heartbreak. I mean, you fall in love with a new sprout after it has budded and blossomed, but autumn comes and there's nothing left but a memory. So you realize that you have got to stay away from the annuals, and concentrate exclusively on the perennials, because that's the only way you'll ever have a stable relationship, year in and year out, if you know what I mean. Sure, the winters are tough, but you can get through it, knowing that the spring is sure to come, and love will once again be in bloom."

"I didn't know we even had a Botanical Garden at the foot of the Capitol," said one congressman. "And if they find out that this is the kind of stuff that goes on there, there's going to be hell to pay, I can tell you that."

"We'll deal with the political consequences later," said Wimbol firmly. "For now, let's just concentrate on our brother's difficulty."

The Director welcomed this brief hiatus in his narrative in order to collect himself. "As I was saying, I knew I had to stick to the perennials, but I lost control of myself when I was wandering among the vines. I fell in love with a watermelon."

"Jiminy Crickets," said Wimbol with a faint whistle. "*That* really is far out, very heavy. A watermelon?"

"Yes," said the Director, "a *Citrullus vulgaris* to be precise. And one thing led to another, as we say; frankly, I didn't know I was capable of such an all-consuming passion."

"Boy," twanged the automobile dealer, "how the hell on God's green earth do you get it goin' with a watermelon? Are you meanin' to say that you made it with a watermelon, that you have really and truly and actually made it with a watermelon, I mean Citrullus vulgaris, or whatever her name was?"

"Well," said the Director, "the sensuous appeal of a firm, well-formed fruit just isn't adequately appreciated. I mean, well, I don't want to get too explicit about this, but, you know, you kind of trace your fingers along the darker green stripes, and then you work your way to the rind, and its slight tartness just prepares you for what lies beyond. And then you savor the seeds one by one, until you're about ready for the point of ecstasy and then, if you've handled the foreplay properly, you mount the watermelon, and it's done."

"Ain't never heard nothin' like that before!" announced the

automobile dealer. "But I suppose there's worse things a man can do."

"Anyway," continued the Director, now starting to appear a bit distraught once again, "I knew we wouldn't have long together, that sooner or later, the inevitable change of the seasons would bring its toll. But I didn't think it would end the way it did, all the fault of my uncontrolled appetites, my irresponsible self-indulgence." At this, the Director began to sob, but he recovered control of himself.

"It happened about a month ago," he continued. "It was a beautiful night, Citrullus and I were there, and we could see the starlight through the roof of the greenhouse. I was never more passionate than I was that night. And I guess I got carried away, because, at the point of climax, I simply didn't realize what I was doing as I clutched Citrullus and, with a violent jerk, detached Citrullus from the vine. When I realized what I had done, I was beside myself; I just lay there, dazed, shocked, overwhelmed with grief. There was Citrullus on the floor of the Botanical Garden, not merely violated, but cut off, cut off forever, from her vital life-support system. I was desperate. I tried to graft her back onto the vine, but I couldn't. I even thought of calling for aid, but I was afraid that what I had been doing would be discovered, and that my career at the agency would be ruined. I mean, the press would have been lurid: 'Twenty-Year Veteran of Agency Rapes Citrullus Vulgaris in Botanical Garden; Attempts to Revive Victim Fail.' I couldn't do it. I just left my Citrullus there on the floor to rot. I was a coward, and I am thoroughly ashamed of myself. I am filled with remorse. I'm starting to drink to excess."

"Yes," said Wimbol, "it reminds me of the line from Oscar Wilde, and Lord knows, he had problems of his own. 'Each man kills the thing he loves . . .'"

"Worse than that," said the Director, "if they ever find out, they'll expel me from the Luther Burbank Society."

The Director was now staring blankly into space. An unaccustomed silence hung over the room. Wimbol sensed that it was time to adjourn the meeting.

It was a month before Wimbol was able to report on the Director's progress. He opened the meeting by reading a letter from the Director to his fellows. "The worst is now over," the Director had written. "A team of agronomists working together with the famous researchers on sexual behavior at Indiana University seem to have discovered that hortosexual impulses can be arrested by massive dosages of vitamin C, and they have prescribed two million units per day for me. As for the guilt, it too will pass, for I shall travel the country planting watermelon seeds wherever I can."

"We ought to be pleased by this," Wimbol said solemnly, after finishing the reading, "for it gives hope to us all. It is living testimony to the redemptive power of love."

Lost Names

One crucial distinction between Washington, D.C., and New York City is that, in Washington, one almost never encounters anyone named Irving. Even in New York, where Irvings almost surely originated, they are becoming a rare breed. The rapid proliferation of Jasons, Scotts, and Michaels threatens to make the Irving an endangered species. This is of substantial interest to students of Americana. Is it really the case that we will come to think of the Irving as a meteor which flashed across the sky, providing brief but intense illumination, then either to burn up or somehow escape the earth's gravitation, so that it will pass into the cosmos? Or will we come to recognize the Irving as a permanent link in the Great Chain of Being?

It fell to the Smithsonian Institution—as is customary in these cases—to fix the Irving firmly in the American tradition. Jason Wilkens, whose father was of course named Irving, had taken the lead in his capacity as Associate Curator of the historical collections. He had pushed through the memorable exhibition "Honor Thy Irving" and had followed it up with the even more widely attended display "A Nation of Irvings." Now he wished to make the Irving a permanent feature of the Museum of History and Technology by opening a Hall of Irvings.

All this was characteristic of the élan and daring that Wilkens had brought to the otherwise stodgy profession of museum administration. Others might seek to reconstruct an ancient Assyrian palace under a plexiglass roof; Wilkens thought in larger, more monumental, indeed genuinely monumental, terms. A living monument to the Irving, now that was something you could sink your teeth into!

Funds earmarked for this purpose were deposited in a special escrow account at the Irving Trust Company in New York City. A Board of Advisers was appointed. Its members included Irving Babbitt, Irving Berlin, Irving Caesar, Irving Crane, Irving Horowitz, Irving Howe, Clifford Irving, Julius Erving, Earvin "Magic" Johnson, Washington Irving, Irving Kristol, Irving Lazar, Irving R. Levine, and Irving Shapiro. The Board held its meetings in a small house in Irvington, New Jersey. It was agreed that a nationwide fund-raising effort would be launched. Sophisticated analysis of computer lists revealed the name of every American who had an uncle named Irving, and they would be contacted directly. It was estimated that $7 million could be raised in this way.

Meanwhile, something else had occurred to Wilkens. One day, he was struck by the curious fact that Levi Strauss the pants maker and Lévi-Strauss the structuralist both had the same name. And yet both Levis and Strausses were in as much peril as Irvings. One thought immediately of Leo Strauss the philosopher and Lewis Strauss, Eisenhower's old friend. One conjured up a mental picture of Bernard-Henri Lévy, the new philosopher, and Seymour Levy, the old baker of rye bread that one needn't be Jewish to love. Were there not almost as many Americans who had an Uncle Levi as an

Uncle Irving? If this were true, one needed only to enlist the political acumen of Robert Strauss and the awesome musical reputation of Richard Strauss to create yet another new Hall in the Smithsonian Institution. But all this was daydreaming, as Wilkens soon realized. He could never get it past his superiors.

Months passed, and the dedication of the new Hall of Irvings was imminent. By passage of a concurrent resolution, Congress established a National Irving Week. The City Council agreed to a special set of traffic regulations so that a block party could be held on Irving Street. The Dallas Cowboys played a special exhibition game in their stadium in Irving, Texas. Rock Creek Park was the site of a gigantic rock concert, followed by a massive gathering known simply as an Irv-In.

Everyone who was anyone in political Washington turned out for the opening. Some came out of polite curiosity, others merely to gawk. And busloads of ordinary Irvings were brought down from New York City—accountants, beer distributors, divorce lawyers, carpet wholesalers, paint salesmen, piano tuners, orthodontists. They were led by Irving and Esther Seligman, who also brought along their daughter Courtney.

It was the most brilliant assemblage of eminent Irvings in a single room since Irving Jefferson dined alone.

Drink American

For the third time in a week, the National Security Council met to grapple with the latest threat to the National Security. The latest statistical evidence had demonstrated that, in the past five years, the nation had become dangerously dependent on imported mineral water. What was once a trickle had become a flood. Ten years ago, only 3 percent of the water swallowed by Americans was imported. Today, it was 53 percent, and that figure was growing. "We have become profligate drinkers of imported water, and unless we move vigorously to ensure our water independence, future generations will be at the mercy of a handful of mineral water exporters—whether they choose to drink it straight or as a mixer with their favorite intoxicant." This was the grim conclusion of the memorandum under discussion.

The fact was that we had failed to move to develop our own supplies of mineral and spring water. Initially, we had turned to France, which was prepared to supply us with water in small green bottles. Then it was Spain, which supplied water in small pink bottles. Finally, it was Germany, which began to export Löwenwasser to the United States in ever-larger quantities. The French, in their typically opportunistic fashion, had chosen to exploit political turmoil on the Continent to their own advantage. But it was not until the French Communist Party attained to power that we felt the full force of the Water Weapon. The French organized the dreaded OMWEC—the Organization of Mineral Water Exporting Countries—and drove the world price of mineral water to a level that no econometric model had ever contemplated.

The President's advisers traced the origins of the new crisis to the Water Import Control Quota Plan of several years ago. Domestic bottlers had demanded a nationwide "Drink American" campaign and had, in a nationwide television campaign, encouraged consumers to boycott the foreign competition. But this produced distortions in the market. Foreign mineral water was, initially, cheaper than domestic water, so that the European exporters gradually developed a stranglehold on our market. Once entrenched, and prodded by the Communists— and by those nations where the annual rainfall was less than three inches per year—the exporters raised prices and reaped enormous profits—waterfall profits, as they were known in the industry.

Why then our dangerous complacency? The President's advisers theorized that it had something to do with the ease with which the notorious oil cartel had crumbled. OPEC, which had held sway for only ten years, collapsed shortly after American scientists had discovered a process which converted cumulus clouds directly into gasoline. After that, no one could be persuaded to take cartels seriously. The constrictions in the market for natural spring water were seen as temporary, more the result of politics than of the laws of supply and demand. Besides, as one expert put it, the world is swimming in water —or we are swimming in a world of water, he had forgotten which; sooner or later the weight of the world's oceans would be brought into play.

Yet that had not happened. The Water Independence Act, which provided huge amounts for desalinization projects, did not have any noticeable effect. Consumers shunned fresh water made from the sea. It was flat in taste, and it was not naturally carbonated, nor did it come from any mysterious spring originating deep within the earth's surface. In fact, no one with any taste would touch the stuff. It was scarcely fit for washing the car.

No, nothing seemed to work. Those who believed that the colored bottles were the secret of foreign water's appeal were disappointed when the stuff was purchased in growing quantities—even after it was imported in supertankers which OMWEC had picked up from OPEC after the latter's demise. Nor was price a factor. Domestic water in most areas sold for less than one dollar per thousand gallons; imported water sold for one dollar for seven ounces. According to the theory of the rational consumer which dominates contemporary economics, a rational man would have gone to his faucet and, for less than a penny, would have drunk enough water to burst his innards. Instead, he preferred to spend two dollars for a quantity of water that could scarcely wet his whistle.

Nor was the Internal Revenue Code the answer. Congress had deliberated long and hard before passing the Excess Effervescence Tax. This levy, which had as its purpose reducing the number of bubbles per bottle in order to make imported water more like domestic water, had little effect. Then there was the Coca-Cola Conversion Act. Its purpose was to offer enormous subsidies to the soft-drink industry to remove the flavoring and color from its products, so as to make them more like imported water. It was also thought that water packaged in cans would have greater appeal than water bottled in bottles. Instead, Americans started to mix Coke syrup with Perrier, creating a new sensation, and driving the demand for imported water even higher.

It had become painfully obvious that the government's

countermeasures had been thwarted at every turn. The trade balance dipped deeper into the red and the dollar plummeted to its lowest levels in history. This was an embarrassment to the President, for it made a mockery of his campaign pledge to restore America to its former greatness. "It is nothing but self-hatred," he had said on the stump. "A nation which will not drink its own water has lost its instinct for self-preservation." And, to underscore his commitment to water independence, the President, as a candidate, had ridden over Niagara Falls in a barrel. "It is time," he had said, "for a National Water Policy as thirsty as the American people themselves."

The only response to that brave call, however, was more of the same. Americans began to make even their ice cubes out of imported natural spring water. It was discovered that if the water were flash-frozen, the bubbles remained embedded in the ice cube, creating an effect that was as pleasing to the eye as to the palate. Then they began to import such ice cubes themselves, neatly packaged, with a small fleur-de-lis running through them, rather than the plain old round hole which was a feature of the mundane ice cube produced in the average American ice-making machine. Then they turned on ice *cubes* altogether, coming to prefer water frozen in the shape of a regular polyhedron. Of these, the ice dodecahedron was the most popular. It revolutionized the highball.

This, then, was the stark reality which hovered over the President and his advisers as they pondered what to do next. As the discussions continued, it was clear that a bitter division existed between the hawks and the doves. The hawks favored reinstating the Eighteenth Amendment with slightly altered wording, so that it would apply to imported water rather than to intoxicants. The doves, on the other hand, favored total deregulation. It was not clear what that meant in the context of water policy, but the doves kept falling back to their point that, whatever it meant, it was surely in keeping with the temper of the times. As usual, the deliberations of the Council were inconclusive, yielding nothing but a decision to convene another meeting.

It was hardly surprising that concerned Americans would take matters into their own hands. There are, after all, abuses which can be tolerated no longer, affronts to the national dignity which must be answered. And so it happened in the dead of night that a band of patriots, dressed in eighteenth-century attire, boarded a freighter of Panamanian registry moored in Boston Harbor, and proceeded to dump case after case of French water into the sea. The Boston Water Party, now an annual tradition more or less, rejoins Americans to their fighting tradition. And it has become a standard around which native-born beer drinkers will surely rally.

The Intrusion of Reality

Some people wonder whether the intricacy of modern machinery has already rendered the political figure obsolete. It is generally known, for example, that the personal touch—the basis for the emergence of the modern politician—has already become superfluous. Presidents and congressmen respond to their mountain of mail by employing computerized letter-writing systems and preprogrammed pens for affixing signatures. Live television is no longer what it was. Few people know that Presidential press conferences are now prerecorded on videotape for broadcast at this time. This allows the President to be seen at 10 P.M. Eastern and Pacific time, 9 P.M. Central and Mountain. Indeed, cable television makes possible the simultaneous broadcast of several different press conferences, each one specially targeted to a preselected viewing audience.

All this is harmless. After all, why shouldn't the President be allowed to watch himself on television in the comfort of his living room, the same way Johnny Carson does? But the recent scandal suggests that things may have gone too far. For the "Grillion Affair" has been something of a shock. How did it happen that a group of determined and resourceful Senate aides were able to hide the fact that their boss, Senator Clyde Grillion, had been dead for three years?

"Clyde Grillion dead?" asked his colleague from the same state. "Dead for three years? It's not possible. Why, I spoke to him on the phone the day before yesterday, and I saw him walking down the corridor not five days ago!"

This manner of stunned disbelief was widely shared. But as the facts of the plot came slowly to light, there was no gainsaying the fact that Grillion had been gone for some time, his presence in the Senate a mirage, a carefully orchestrated illusion, achieved by the masterful manipulation of machinery—and a bit of human ingenuity, to be fair.

It was a typical day three years ago. Grillion's driver arrived at his home. He knocked on the door. Receiving no response, he let himself in, and was shocked to discover the Senator dead on the living-room floor. The driver immediately called the Senator's Press Secretary. "I suppose you'll want to be getting out a statement on this," said the driver. "Don't do anything until you hear from me," answered the Press Secretary. "We have to decide how to play it."

The Press Secretary brought the news to the Senator's Principal Assistant. "We can hold the press off for a while," said the Press Secretary, "but they'll be wanting a statement."

"Hmm," said the Principal Assistant, "this is a little inconvenient. We've got the farmers coming in at ten, and the women's group scheduled for eleven. If we cancel the women again, they're going to be mighty upset. It will be the third time their appointment has been canceled, and I'm not sure how they'll take it. Meanwhile, call up the driver and tell him to take the Senator to the committee hearing scheduled for nine-thirty and to put him in his customary chair. The boss never asks questions at committee hearings, so no one is likely to notice. At about nine-fifty, we'll arrange for the messenger to go to the committee room and whisper in the Senator's ear. Then we'll escort him to the office and put him behind his desk for his ten o'clock appointment. If we can get by the farmers, we'll do the same for the women at eleven. Then they'll finally be off our back."

"Smart, real smart," said the Press Secretary admiringly. He conveyed the instructions.

Fortunately, there was nothing scheduled for the afternoon, and they were able to get through the first day without even a minor crisis. "The problem now," said the Principal Assistant, "is whether or not we can sustain the momentum we have established. Just like in football, momentum is everything in politics. If we use our heads, we can probably get through the end of the session, compile an impressive record, and get us re-elected."

The Press Secretary was skeptical. Like all political operatives, he too always used the term "we" or "us" when he meant "he" or "him." A common Washington linguistic habit. "How are you going to vote?" one aide would ask another. "We are going to vote 'no'" would be the reply. Or: "We are going to duck this one." But even though this tradition of discourse was well established, the Press Secretary wondered whether or not it ought to be taken all that literally. But, on sober reflection, the Press Secretary understood that the Principal Assisant was quite correct. "Yes," he said, "there's more of us than there is of him, so why shouldn't we continue to operate as we always have in the past."

Pleased with how well they were managing, the assistants gave themselves raises—that is, the automatic preprogrammed pen signed Grillion's name to the appropriate forms. The remaining time in the session was given over to a congressional junket. "We'll lay on a tour of thirty-seven countries to last about four months, and then we'll be home free until the end of the year," said the Principal Assistant.

To the great relief of the Department of State, Grillion's junket did not result in the sort of embarrassing gaffe the Foreign Service had come to expect. The Principal Assistant to the Secretary of State called the Principal Assistant to the Senator, thanking him for ensuring correct diplomatic behavior during the Senator's mission. "You know," said the Foreign Service officer, "we've heard nothing but praise for the Senator's calm response to persistent anti-American provocation. Even when he was kidnapped by the guerrillas for thirty-seven hours, he remained serene."

"Growth and maturity," said the Principal Assistant. "Senator Grillion now knows how to exercise his enormous power in a measured and precise way."

The Principal Assistant realized, however, that things would be more difficult in the next session. He got into contact with Political Post-Technotronics, Inc., a firm which specialized in the creation of new devices to make the politician's job easier.

"I have a real challenge for you," said the Principal Assistant. "We're discovering that it's hard for the Senator to be at two different places at the same time, and we want to create the impression that he's in the room when really he isn't. What can you do about that?"

"Holographs" was the reply. "A holograph," continued the explanation, "is a kind of three-dimensional photograph made with laser light. We can very easily make a holograph for you and project it into the chair of your choice. To all appearances, it will seem that the Senator is sitting in the chair, but of course he won't be. He will be someplace else."

"You bet," said the Principal Assistant.

Needless to say, the device worked like a charm. A holograph projector was installed in the office, and constituents always emerged from their meetings with the Senator in a positive frame of mind. "He just has a special glow around him," one of them had said. "Maybe that's what they mean by charisma."

Not that problems did not crop up from time to time. After all, people would remark that the Senator would not say much during these meetings, even though he appeared to be very interested in what was being said to him. But, once again, Political Post-Technotronics had the answer. As the vice-president for Research and Development in the firm put it: "We can provide you with a small computerized talking machine that we can place under the chair in which the holograph sits. We can preprogram responses to every conceivable question, about every conceivable issue. We can even arrange for the holograph to speak in six languages if you like."

Now this, thought the Principal Assistant, was a good break. Whenever he escorted a visitor into the Senator's office, he would caution the guest to relax and to be at ease. "You can speak slowly and precisely to the Senator," he would say, "just like you speak to the microwave oven in your very own kitchen." And, in truth, people can become so accustomed to this mode of speech that it became virtually habitual with them.

"My, oh my," cooed one suburban housewife, "the Senator is certainly articulate. He speaks as well as my automatic dryer." And foreigners were also impressed. The French Ambassador marveled that Grillion spoke the perfect Parisian variety of his native tongue. "He'd never be taken for an American," the Ambassador had said admiringly.

And so the office settled into an ongoing routine. Political Post-Technotronics, in a new breakthrough, was able to produce a motion-picture machine which could project holographs. Every so often, the projector would be taken out into the corridor, so that Grillion could be seen walking about, as active as you and me.

This might have gone on indefinitely, were it not for the violent temper of a certain umbrella manufacturer. The officers of the Umbrella Manufacturers Association of America called on Grillion to present their case that they were being driven to the wall by cheap foreign imports. It was on that day that the miniaturized speaking device hidden beneath the holograph's chair somehow malfunctioned. It appeared as if the Senator would respond in nothing but Armenian. "I've had it," said one of the delegation angrily. "The man can't tell the difference between an umbrella manufacturer and a rug merchant!" Thus enraged, he charged at the Senator with an umbrella. As could be expected, he thrust the pointed umbrella right through the holographic image, making nothing but a hole in the leather chair.

"Just as I have always suspected," said the umbrella maker. "There's no substance to this man whatsoever!" And he stormed out in disgust. Unfortunately, he told his story to the press, which managed to figure out that something was amiss.

Thus did the scandal come to light. The Principal Assistant and the Press Secretary were placed under arrest, though it was not obvious what crime they should be charged with. The Press Secretary turned state's evidence, and cut a separate deal with the Justice Department in return for a suspended sentence.

The Principal Assistant, however, was determined to carry his battle through the courts. But as legal fees mounted, he decided in favor of plea bargaining instead. He was sentenced to ninety days—after pleading guilty to eleven counts of being an accessory to politics.

The Morning Ride
of Larethan Wimbol

It was a fine and sunny day, the last day of the current session, and Senator Wimbol decided to drive to work. Even in his one hundred and forty-sixth year, he often drove to work, though some experts on English usage would say that he drove frequently to work. He would drive down the hill, past the farms that had become the estates of the rich which had then been subdivided to become the homes of the middle class. He would drive under the hanging elms, elms holding their memories unto themselves, saying nothing, but looking up toward the clouds even as they hung down, as if to say what they had known of life, and what it meant to be a survivor, a survivor of Dutch elm disease. Then Wimbol would come to an intersection. If the light was red, he would stop; but if it was green, he would go.

He would observe the traffic light as its colors alternated with impudent predictability, first green, then orange, then red, or vice versa. What was the secret of its mysterious power, such that it could command the cars either to stop or to go? The light had never said, uncaring, impersonal machine that it was. It too kept its secrets unto itself, and would not share them, not even with the lamppost. Green. Orange. Red. Not even the three primary colors. And thus there was something artificial about the light. Red. Green. *Blue.* Why had not the inventor of traffic lights employed the primary colors? Curious.

Then Wimbol would drive on. He would drive past the church whose nursery school and day-care center were buried in its basement, a basement which clasped its charges to its breast, so that the children might nurse at the teat of religion even as their natural mothers drove on, further into the town. And he would stop, but only if the light were red.

He would drive on, into the town, with its colors and cameras, with its dancing lights and religious mystics, and then he would turn onto the expressway. The expressway. Nestled close to the Potomac River, close enough to see its own reflection in the water, if only its eyes had not been blinded by its own self-preoccupation, its narcissism, its smugness. Yes, it had been blinded by years of sorrow, but it had decided to tell no one about them. The expressway, too, clutched its secrets beneath itself, such that thousands of commuters might drive over them, never knowing what secrets were suspended beneath. For few ever drove beneath the expressway, even thought it was an elevated highway. And those who did never bothered to look up, for their eyes were always turned to the sidewalk, looking for legal parking spaces.

Wimbol would listen to the car radio as he drove. He would listen to the news and the weather—no secrets there—or so it seemed. And he would wonder, though, what secrets the news would give if it could, if it cared, if it knew—which, of course, it did not. And then he would remember what his grandfather had said. "No news is good news." And a sense of well-being would spread throughout Wimbol's body. He wondered: "Why has it never been said that no weather is good weather? That no sports is good sports? That no traffic report is a good traffic report?" Wimbol resolved to determine whether these things had ever been said. And if they had never been said, he would say them.

It had taken Wimbol many years to acquire a sense of the silence of his surroundings. The city had changed much in the one hundred and fourteen years he had been there. In those days, it had been known for its silent noisiness, which had come to be replaced by a noisy silence. Or was it the other way round? He recalled that a poem had been written about this, about the river that wound its way through the city, and then he realized that the poem he had in mind was Vachel Lindsay's "The Congo," which had little or nothing to do with the separation of powers.

As he tapped out the rhythm of the famous poem on the dashboard—it was a good poem, even if it was not about Washington—he drove on. He came, finally, to the door of the parking garage, and was granted admission to its inner precincts and to its parallel white lines. If those lines knew anything, they weren't saying.

Since it was such a fine day, Wimbol decided to walk to his office in the daylight, rather than use the underground tunnel. As he walked he heard the sound of small-arms fire and the occasional pop of a mortar. Nothing unusual there. Probably just the mopping-up operations. He remembered that the government, in desperation, had called in a brigade of French-speaking paratroopers to restore order, to free the hostages, to disperse the invading force which had seized the town and closed down the copper mines. No, that was not it. "The Congo." By Vachel Lindsay. That was it. He realized he was growing old. He was having a hell of a time keeping his metaphors straight.

Wimbol went to his office. He said good morning to the receptionist, and then he said good morning to his secretary. His secretary, Sister Thomas, was a nun who had been granted a special fellowship by the convent to work for a year in a government office. She was very efficient and a stickler for detail. Wimbol, though a Protestant, enjoyed being the only senator who had a nun for his personal secretary. Sister Thomas, in her striking habit, would swish through the office. She also taught Wimbol how to diagram sentences.

Sister Thomas would bring Senator Wimbol a cup of coffee. Then the two of them would play their morning game of cat's cradle. The string was kept in the right-hand drawer of Wimbol's desk, and only the two of them knew where it was. Sometimes they would play checkers. But they never played Scrabble, because Sister Thomas was too good at it. But this morning was different. Senator Wimbol played by himself. A toy manufacturer had sent him its very successful toy, Electronic Congress, and Wimbol enjoyed pushing the buttons, watching the lights, and listening to the beeping noises. It all seemed so simple. He longed for a time when life had been more complicated.

Sometimes another senator would call on the telephone:

—Good morning, Larethan.
—Good morning, James.
—Fine day.
—Very.
—I'm lonely.
—Why?
—No one will co-sponsor my bill.
—Don't be lonely. I'll co-sponsor your bill.
—Will you?
—Yes.
—Then I won't be lonely.
—Yes. I'll be your friend.
—Larethan?
—Yes, James.
—Do you love me?
—Only on Thursdays.
—Larethan?

—Yes, James.
—Do you record your telephone conversations?
—Yes.
—Why?
—Because I want to publish them in *The New Yorker*.
—Near a cognac ad?
—Close, but not next to.
—Is there another reason?
—Yes.
—What is it?
—I want to prove that people can still communicate.
—Can they, Larethan?
—Yes, James. Sister Thomas told me.
—Goodbye, Larethan.
—Goodbye, James.

Senator Wimbol would then answer a few letters, and it would be time for lunch. After lunch, Senator Wimbol would take a nap. He always dreamed the same dream. He would dream that he was a member of the United States Olympic team and that he had just done thirty-three feet two inches in the existential leap. But as the gold medal was about to be hung around his neck, the ribbon would begin to strangle him. The ribbon was always a long sentence with subordinate clauses. Then he would wake up.

After his nap, Wimbol would work hard throughout the afternoon. At about five-thirty, he would reflect on what he had accomplished, and he would be pleased. Today was no different.

He had done well. He wanted a smoke.